125 Tested Techniques
for Classroom Management
& Control

TEACHER SMART!

125 Tested Techniques for Classroom Management & Control

GEORGE WATSON

Illustrated by Allan Anthony

THE CENTER FOR APPLIED
RESEARCH IN EDUCATION
West Nyack, New York 10994

Library of Congress Cataloging-in-Publication Data

Watson, George
      Teacher smart!   :   125 tested techniques for classroom management
and control / by George Watson   ;   illustrated by Alan Anthony.
          p.   cm.
      ISBN 0–87628–910–3 (S)   ISBN 0–87628–913–8 (P)
      1. Classroom management.   I. Title.
LB3013.W38   1996
371.1'024—dc20   96–894
                                                                            CIP

Printed in the United States of America

10 9 8 7 6 5 4 3 2 1

ISBN 0-87628-910-3 (S)   ISBN 0-87628-913-8 (P)

┌───┐

ATTENTION: CORPORATIONS AND SCHOOLS

The Center for Applied Research in Education books are available at quantity discounts with bulk purchase for educational, business, or sales promotional use. For information, please write to: Prentice Hall Career & Personal Development Special Sales, 113 Sylvan Avenue, Englewood Cliffs, NJ 07632. Please supply: title of book, ISBN, quantity, how the book will be used, date needed.

└───┘

**THE CENTER FOR APPLIED RESEARCH
IN EDUCATION**
West Nyack, NY 10994
A Simon & Schuster Company

On the World Wide Web at http://www.phdirect.com

Prentice Hall International (UK) Limited, *London*
Prentice Hall of Australia Pty. Limited, *Sydney*
Prentice Hall Canada, Inc., *Toronto*
Prentice Hall Hispanoamericana, S.A., *Mexico*
Prentice Hall of India Private Limited, *New Delhi*
Prentice Hall of Japan, Inc., *Tokyo*
Simon & Schuster Asia Pte. Ltd., *Singapore*
Editora Prentice Hall do Brasil, Ltda., *Rio de Janeiro*

This book is dedicated to my wife, Kathy,
and to my two children, Christa and Tony.

ACKNOWLEDGMENTS

My Parents—Alberta & John Watson

Alan Anthony

Diane & Gene Aulinger

Linda & Marvin Brose

Barb Campbell

Bill Cowan

Linda Davisson

Lorraine & Ed Feigal

Mrs. Foucheau

Joe Fransoo

Cam Gjosund

Merv Grosse

Phyllis Gruending

Karen Guenther

John Hall

Greg Harnet

Rose Harnet

Irene & Pat Heffernan

John Hunchak

Esther Johnson

Don Johnston

Jack Jones

Susan Kachur

Alice Kadun

Ben Kirkpatrick

Fred Kozakewich

James Carl Lindgren

Ann Marie Merle

Paul Nickel

Laurie Nyholt

Owen O'Donavon

Jack Peters

Dennis Poulin

George Ridley

Randy Rodger

Barb Sealy

Sister Zelie

Cliff Stade

Art Tegart

George Thompson

Diane & Jim Tiessen

Gordon Waldner

Audrey & Jake Wall

Ilene Wettergreen

Ann Marie Woytowich

Louise & Dick Zentner

Steve & Brent Zurevinski

ABOUT THE AUTHOR

George Watson (B.A., University of Saskatchewan, Saskatoon, Saskatchewan, Canada) has taught almost every subject including major academic subjects, physical education and art at the elementary and junior high school levels during 22 years of teaching. He currently teaches grades eight and nine and special education at Alexander Junior High School in the North Battleford (Saskatchewan) Public School Division. He conducts in-service programs for teachers; he is also an author of short stories that are published in Canadian magazines as well as a book on hot rodding.

ABOUT THIS RESOURCE

The tricks of the trade that teachers develop out of many years of experience can be very helpful to new teachers and also to other veteran teachers. I started creating techniques in behavior management, troubleshooting, stress management, communication, and other kinds of efficiencies as a social worker over twenty years ago and have continued to do this in my teaching career. To ensure the success of the students I'm now teaching on the junior high level, I developed and wrote a special program and applied for an educational grant from the Canadian Federal Government. Because of this experience, I've been asked to present area inservices to share my practical working ideas with other teachers. These sessions have been quite rewarding to all of us. Teachers literally have clamored for more.

Their excitement helped me realize that a vacuum exists in the area of positive practical ideas for the whole classroom. I began to compile all my "tricks" into a manuscript—which has become the resource you're now holding in your hands. So to everyone who is faced with a barrage of daily pressures, manipulations, and frustrations along with the rewards of teaching, help is here.

Each of the seven sections in this resource focuses on a different area of concern—behavior control, reinforcement and rewards, on-task behavior, neat and fun things to do in school, communication and professional ideas, self-esteem, and teacher and student protection. Each idea or concept within each section identifies a specific problem in the teacher's environment and offers a well-tested solution. More than half of these solutions include a form or chart that can be reproduced as many times as needed for an entire class, thus saving time as well as solving a problem.

Section 1 deals with problems of behavior control that most teachers see every day. It shows techniques that are effective and inexpensive such as "Dueling Pens," a way to quickly stop a squabble in the classroom. In another idea, students actually deliver themselves to the office or to another classroom when they are causing trouble. These and other behavior control ideas allow teachers the freedom that comes from a well-controlled classroom with a positive atmosphere.

Section 2 shows how to use positive reinforcement to produce results. "Percent Ticket," for example, is a no-cost idea to help all students improve and increase day-to-day class work. Other teachers who have used it agree that it works great!

Novel ideas to keep students working on task can be found in Section 3. One of these, "The Stick Jar," keeps students on their toes because they never know when their name will be drawn from the jar. This and other ideas help keep students working and aware of their performance all the time.

This resource also provides ways of injecting some good old-fashioned fun into the classroom. Section 4 reveals many creative things to do in today's classroom, which, in effect, reduce stress by making the teacher's day just that much more pleasant. "The Great Impromptu Speech" requires little if any preparation, lasts a whole school period, and keeps even students with the most difficult behavior problems alert and learning. This section contains a wealth of other original ideas that are truly neat and fun to do.

To help the staff interact and communicate in their working environment, Section 5 covers positive interaction with others in the school environment. It provides communication tools, basic forms teachers need, ideas for substitute teachers, a really neat teacher stress reducer called "The Colorful Generic Lesson Plan File," and other professional ideas.

Section 6 was designed to help teachers promote compassionate self-esteem. It includes seven meaningful ideas for students' emotional development. These imaginative concepts apply to the broad range of students in the academic spectrum. We sometimes inadvertently neglect the bright students in terms of positive reinforcement. The ideas in this area can be used for everyone because all students need to feel good.

Suggestions to help teachers protect themselves and their students are another unique advantage of this resource. In a time when teachers are feeling increasing demands and expectations, they sometimes take the blame for student-centered inconsistencies. The idea called "Refusal Protection" in Section 7 puts the ownership for poor school performance directly where it belongs, on the student. With this, the teacher is shielded from parent and student criticisms because the student describes the circumstance for his or her refusal to take a test. The student, in effect, admits responsibility for non-test performance.

Another idea in this section includes a form that can be very handy when parents query why a particular grade is low. The form proves that the poor performance is completely the student's responsibility.

This resource effectively opens my classroom and my experience to all teachers to help them create a positive atmosphere that they and their students will look forward to sharing every day.

George T. Watson

CONTENTS

★ 2 ★

REINFORCEMENT AND REWARD SYSTEMS—47

GRADE LEVEL BEST
SUITED FOR

★ **3** ★

ON-TASK BEHAVIOR—69

GRADE LEVEL BEST
SUITED FOR

⋆ 5 ⋆

COMMUNICATION AND PROFESSIONAL IDEAS—161

GRADE LEVEL BEST
SUITED FOR

⋆ 1 ⋆

BEHAVIOR CONTROL

Learning cannot be accomplished in an undisciplined environment. Teachers are required to maintain control of their classrooms at all times. This is still true even in an era when teachers' disciplinary parameters are more and more restricted. Teachers need strong behavior control ideas that are legal, nondemeaning and effective. This Behavior Control section is jampacked with creative concepts that fulfill these criteria.

1. SELF-REMOVING BEHAVIOR PROBLEMS

Problem: Sometimes in the hustle and bustle of your classroom, a behavior problem student will do his or her best to disrupt the proceedings. (Sound familiar?)

This is especially true if in the normal course of events you cannot keep an eye on this particular student one hundred percent of the time.

How do you remove the behavior problem from your midst in the quickest and most efficient way possible? How do you avoid a confrontation with the behavior problem child while removing him or her from the class?

Solution: Write the following message on a note, "This student is causing a disturbance in my classroom. Please keep him/her in the office until I am able to talk to this child."

Seal the note in an official-looking envelope on which you have written, "Please give the student a response." You now ask for a volunteer (if you think your problem student would volunteer) to take the letter to the office. If you feel the student would not normally volunteer, then just send the child with the letter.

You tell the student not to return to class until he or she has obtained a response from the office.

The behavior problem child will thus successfully transport him- or herself to the office to deal with the consequences he or she deserves.

In order for this idea to work, it is necessary for you to have the prearranged cooperation of your school's central office.

If office support is not available, it is possible to make an arrangement with a colleague in another classroom. You can send your behavior problem to that other cooperating teacher, thus putting the student out of the environment of his or her peers.

If you are cooperating with another teacher on this, it means you will probably have to accept a behavior problem child from that other class; therefore, you should keep a desk in a corner of your room for this purpose.

2. PARAMETERS WITH POWER

Problem: You have a hyperkinetic child in your classroom. You want this child to learn as much as he or she can while you are both trying to maintain control over the hyperactivity.

You know you must create the maximum learning environment for the hyper child at the same time you create the maximum learning environment for the twenty-plus other eager minds in your charge. How do you help the hyperkinetic youngster feel secure and develop self-esteem, as you give equal billing to the other children?

Solution 1: The hyperkinetic child needs well-defined parameters, not well defined lectures like "sit still" or "stop moving around."

You must set limits on the spacial movements of the hyper child. These limits or parameters must be set up by you in a fair, compassionate, and yet, concrete way. These parameters are made by placing a rectangle or square of masking tape on the floor around the desk of the hyper student. The tape should extend out about one foot beyond the desk of the student. You then tell the hyperkinetic student that this is his or her personal space. That student now owns the space. The student can move as much as he or she wants within the space he or she owns, but cannot leave that space without the teacher's permission.

Likewise, other students cannot enter the space without the direct consent of the student owner of the space.

© 1996 by The Center for Applied Research in Education

These parameters define a safe island for this child. Ownership gives him or her a degree of power over his or her environment. From this develops important benefits in the areas of self-esteem and social skills.

The hyperkinetic youngster may do somersaults within the boundaries of the parameters, but you will find that the child will not leave the space. The strongly defined limits will help this often-apprehensive student feel secure in the classroom.

With this idea, you will successfully tame the classroom for the hyperactive student and for the twenty-plus other students you need to teach.

Solution #2: The Two-Desk Parameter With Power System. Have two desks for the hyperactive student. Place these desks at the rear of the classroom but on opposite sides. You need as much room between them as circumstance will allow. Place a straight line of masking tape on the floor from one desk to the other.

Give the student these instructions, "These are your two desks. One is Desk 'A' and the other is Desk 'B'. Whenever I see you, you must be in Desk 'A' or 'B' or somewhere traveling in between. You cannot stop on the masking tape line without my permission."

When the student feels the urge to become mobile, he or she now has a socially acceptable way of doing this. The student can travel from one desk to another without incurring the wrath of the teacher or interfering with other students.

This sets limits on the mobility of the child as well as allowing the necessary amount of freedom for the student to "blow off a little steam" when he or she needs to.

The other students quickly learn to adapt and enjoy the "Two-Desk Parameter System" because it makes the classroom more predictable for them also.

3. DUELING PENS

Problem: You have two students fighting over a pen. The squabble is fairly intense and it is difficult for you to discern who is the rightful owner of the pen or pencil. Problems like this, while minor, have exploded into larger confrontations that involve parents.

Solution: When you have two students fighting over a pen, you take the pen. Give each of the students a pen from your teacher's supply. Tell the students that at the end of the day or period the rightful owner of the pen can come to claim it.

By the time school or the period is over, tempers have calmed down and life will have returned to normal. Most likely the original rightful owner of the pen will come to claim it. There is a good chance neither student will come to you to get the pen. The point here is that you diffused the situation. That is what you wanted to do.

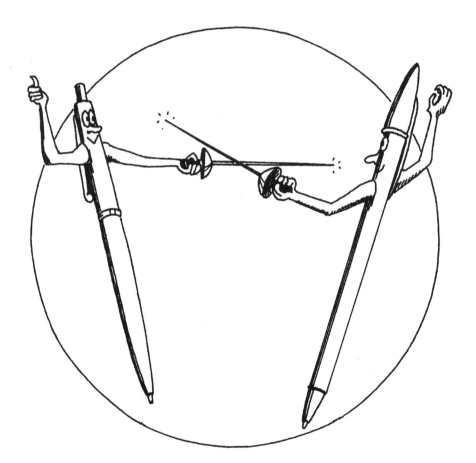

4. COOPERATIVE BEHAVIOR MONITOR NOTICE

Problem: It seems like the homeroom class 8A is on a poor behavior binge. It does occur that certain classes will take a behavior turn for the worse. The problem becomes especially acute when that class moves from one room to another to take different subjects. The poor behavior dynamics of the class then become every teacher's problem. How do we control the poor behavior of a class that is taught by more than one teacher?

Solution: This idea requires a coordinated effort by your staff plus leadership or ownership by a teacher, principal or guidance counselor who acts as a control leader.

Photocopy Figure 1–1 and glue or laminate it onto a stiff piece of cardboard.

Figure 1–1 states *"Class _____'s behavior is being monitored today. If its behavior as a group is poor, please inform the control leader who will deal with the problem. If you would like to add extra work because of their behavior, please feel free to do so.*

The home telephone number of any student in this class is immediately available upon request.

Please display this sign in a prominent place where all members of the class may see it while they are being taught by you."

The sign of course is self explanatory and has its own momentum if the control person is able to back it up with action.

You will need to assign one reliable student to carry the sign from class to class. This monitor board gives the students a continuous present consciousness of their behavior. It instantly informs other teachers of the need to correct the class's behavior. The behavior monitor board adds to inter-teacher communication and reinforces the truism that if one teacher sees the need to change the behavior of a class, most likely other teachers will have noticed the same thing.

(Figure 1–1)

BEHAVIOR MONITOR NOTICE

CLASS _____'S BEHAVIOR IS BEING MONITORED TODAY. IF THEIR BEHAVIOR AS A GROUP IS POOR, PLEASE INFORM THE CONTROL LEADER WHO WILL DEAL WITH THE PROBLEM.

IF YOU WOULD LIKE TO ADD EXTRA WORK BECAUSE OF THEIR BEHAVIOR, PLEASE FEEL FREE TO DO SO. THE HOME TELEPHONE NUMBER OF ANY STUDENT IN THIS CLASS IS IMMEDIATELY AVAILABLE UPON REQUEST.

PLEASE DISPLAY THIS NOTICE IN A PROMINENT PLACE WHERE ALL MEMBERS OF THE CLASS MAY SEE IT WHILE THEY ARE BEING TAUGHT BY YOU.

5. IT'S A NO HAT, NO GUM AND NO CANDY ENVIRONMENT

Problem: Students like chewing gum, wearing hats and eating loads of candy. This is a reality that no teacher likes to see come into the classroom.

What can you use as a constant reminder to the students that you do not tolerate gum, hats or candy in your work area?

Solution: Use the no hat, no gum and no candy signs provided (Figures 1–2, 1–3 and 1–4).

These signs are black and white and are therefore very noticeable. They can be seen quite well if they are placed in strategic locations in the classroom and hallways. One of the best locations is on the outside of the classroom door. As a student enters class, he or she is reminded that your teaching area is a no hat, no gum, and no candy environment.

(Figure 1–2)

THIS IS A
NO

ENVIRONMENT

(Figure 1–3)

THIS IS A
NO

ENVIRONMENT

(Figure 1–4)

THIS IS A
NO

ENVIRONMENT

6. THE CLASSIC FIVE-MINUTE WASHROOM CONTROL TECHNIQUE

Problem: Most students who ask to leave the class to use the washroom facilities genuinely do need to; however, there are a few students who ask to go to the washroom who do not need to go at all. They are either trying to avoid in-class work or they want to fool around in the hall or washroom.

You, as a teacher, are in a double bind situation here. You have no way of telling whether a student really needs to go or not. To deny a request for washroom privileges could spell disaster as you well know and by the same token to let a student wander the halls avoiding work is also wrong. How do you stop or prevent abuse of washroom privileges while allowing for genuine needs in this area?

Solution: When a student, whom you suspect of being a washroom rights offender, asks you to let him or her go, you say to that student "Yes, you may go but not right now. Ask me again in five minutes."

The results will amaze you. If the student really needed to go, he or she will ask you again in two to five minutes. If that child didn't need to go to the washroom, he or she will most likely forget about it.

13

7. A VIDEO FOR MOM AND DAD

Problem: You want to show the parents of your students exactly how those students learn and behave in class.

You believe parents want to know firsthand what is happening to their child.

You would like to present a totally unique experience for parents on "Meet the Teacher Night."

How do you most effectively show parents how their children learn and behave while in your charge?

Solution: Videotape the students in your class as they go through a normal learning day.

It is best to set the video camera up ahead of time for younger students to become used to it and its function.

The videotaping must be done with the complete knowledge and approval of the parents and the students. The rights of the students being videotaped must be respected at all times. We provide a Videotape Permission Form for this purpose (Figure 1–5).

Once the camera has been around for a while, the students will consider it to be part of the furniture and will act totally naturally, thus allowing you to get as true a picture as possible of the students' performance. The camera allows you to show parents how their children learn in the classroom setting as compared with other places. You will find that many parents will be thrilled to see how terrific their child is in school. If you capture poor behavior by a student, it may or may not be advantageous to show this. This will, of course, be your discretionary call at that time. Remember, the rights of students' parents and the rules of your school environment must be regarded at all times.

The videotape can be a learning tool for the students as well. When they see themselves, they will be able to pick out habits or interaction situations they personally would like to improve upon.

(Figure 1–5)

VIDEOTAPE PERMISSION FORM

Teacher's name: _____   Class name: _____

Date(s) of Videotaping: _____

I hereby give permission for my child _____
(first and last name)

to be videotaped as part of a normal school day in the classroom.

I understand I will be able to view the videotape at school upon request.

_____   _____
Date   Parent(s)/Guardian(s) Signature

8. GETTING A HANDLE ON A LINE

Problem: Many teachers fall victim to the sheer volume of students that are in many classes today. Work must be corrected and checked for every student even in the largest classes.

If the teacher allows a line to form at his or her desk for the purpose of doing that correcting or checking of work, he or she ends up with a logistical problem at two distinct places because the line will obstruct the teacher's view of the classroom proceedings.

There will be a problem of students fooling around in the line itself and the students at their desks will tend to be disruptive as well when they think they cannot be seen by the teacher. How does the teacher maintain control when correcting, checking and giving individual instruction to one student after another at that teacher's desk?

Solution: This idea takes a page from those supermarket or hardware lines where people are served in the chronological order of tickets as they are taken by the customers from a dispenser.

There are two basic approaches to implementing this in the classroom.

In the first system you will need a jar or a box with as many tickets or cards as you have students in the classroom. (I prefer laminated cards because they are more durable.) The cards or tickets are numbered in sequence, 1, 2, 3, 4, . . . and so forth. As students finish their work they take a ticket. You call up the students to your desk in the number sequence you desire (usually chronologically). Only one or two numbers are called at a time, thus causing only one or two students to be at the teacher's desk at a time.

The students would normally keep their numbered cards at their desk until the end of the period. This would avoid confusion if a card number was returned to the box and another student would take it and therefore not get the work corrected because the teacher had already served that number.

The second way to operate a card or ticket system is to have a jar, box or even a pocket on a bulletin board or other convenient place with only two or three tickets or cards in the pocket. When students need work corrected, they take a ticket and come up to you while holding the ticket. When his or her business at the teacher's desk is finished, the student returns the ticket or card to the pocket or jar. Other students who need tickets take them as they become available.

The beauty of these numbered card or ticket systems is that they control the quantity of students at the teacher's desk at one time. Once the students get on to the system, it will become second nature to them. Therefore, in effect, the students end up controlling their own behavior. The long line will be gone and students' work will be viewed and corrected in an efficient manner.

© 1996 by The Center for Applied Research in Education

9. THE HALL PASS

Problem: Some students are seen in the hall outside the classroom while their class is in session.

A teacher seeing these students does not know whether they should be there or not. If the teacher queries the student or students as to why they are in the hall during class times, he or she will no doubt get a response but the teacher has no real way of verifying the answer the student gives.

How do you control aimless wandering of students in the halls of your school? How do you provide those students, who genuinely have a reason to be in the hall, with some kind of concrete proof of their right to be there?

Solution: Make two or three Hall Passes (Figure 1–6) for each room. When it is necessary for a student to leave the room, the student must take the hall pass with him or her.

The passes themselves are to be placed conveniently by the door on a nail or hook so all that is necessary is for the students to grab the pass on the way out. After they have performed their necessary task out of the classroom, they simply return the hall pass to its location near the door.

If a student in the hall is confronted by a teacher or other school staff member, a quick flash of the Hall Pass by the student will indicate to the staff member that this student has a legitimate reason to be where he or she is.

The giving out of the Hall Pass is purely a discretionary call on the part of the classroom teacher. The teacher would have the power to either give the pass to one person or to the leader of a group of students who must stay together.

Two or three Hall Passes is usually the most workable number for the average classroom. If you only have one, then it becomes restrictive, especially when you have those dire emergencies that seem to crop up so often.

To use more than three Hall Passes could cause you problems in terms of having too many students out of the class at one time. Two or three passes seem to work well.

Hall Passes can be color coded for each classroom. This will allow any of the school staff to know at a glance which classroom the students are from. You may wish to have 'special' Hall Passes. These would allow students to be in certain rooms of the school only if they have the special Hall Pass.

The Hall Pass provides you with a reasonable assurance that a student has a legitimate reason to be where he or she is. It allows you to control the number of students who are out of the room for any given amount of time and it will make nonregistered 'students' think twice before entering the halls of your school.

(Figure 1–6)

10. A SOLUTION TO THE CHRONIC ATTENTION-SEEKER PROBLEM

Problem: There are some students who are constantly coming up to you for reaffirmation or reassurance. Some students have insecurities in their lives and will latch onto you because you represent stability.

If you keep responding to this child's questions and need for reassurance, you will not get much work done, nor will you be able to give the other students the time they deserve. This is a very difficult situation because you do not want to be mean or coercive toward the insecure student but you must be free to help all the children.

How do you wean the chronic attention seeker from this behavior without increasing his or her problem in the area?

Solution: Use a deck of playing cards as a behavior control system. At the start of each week, give this student half of a deck of playing cards. This is a selected set of twenty-six cards. Tell the student that each card has a face value according to the number or figure on the card. An ace is worth one point, a deuce is worth two points, right up to a King or Queen as the high cards worth twelve points.

You tell the student that every time he or she seeks attention for something that is not part of the normal routine, he or she must give you back a card. The more frivolous the reason (at your discretion), the higher the value of the card he or she must give back to you. Tell the student you will provide a reward at the end of the week or month that must be purchased with the points remaining. The more points the student has saved by not coming up to you for nonimportant reasons, the better the reward that can be purchased.

Remember, this behavior modification system is only going to work if there is commitment. You create that commitment by providing meaningful, consistent rewards for the student.

This program is designed to give the student some ownership of the problem and the solution to that problem. But remember, sensitivity and discernment on the teacher's part is most important here. A working quality relationship can be the result with the student being the maximum benefactor.

11. THE TWO-WEEK NOTICE IDEA

Problem: Students tend to forget certain upcoming events, such as tests, field trips, concerts and sporting activities.

How can you keep the students and their families constantly aware of upcoming events?

Solution: Send home the Two-Week Notice Sheet (Figure 1–7) that is specific to your class. This sheet outlines exactly which events will be taking place in the next two weeks that are of relevance to your classroom. This tool can be used by you to target those things from which you need feedback or preparation from the students. Test deadlines and term paper due dates are prime examples. If whole school events dovetail with the happenings of your class, you may wish to include these items.

This notice is a great help to the parents of today. Many households are busy at meal times, for example, with parents and students going every which way.

It might be convenient for you to attach a permission or volunteer request form to this Two-Week Notice Sheet. It will be sure to get attention.

Ideally, students should be told to place the notice on the family refrigerator door where all are certain to see it.

(Figure 1–7)

THE TWO-WEEK NOTICE FORM

Teacher: _____

Student: _____   Grade: _____   Room: _____

Week of _____ to _____	Week of _____ to _____
Monday _____	Monday _____
Tuesday _____	Tuesday _____
Wednesday _____	Wednesday _____
Thursday _____	Thursday _____
Friday _____	Friday _____

12. BRING IN MOM

Problem: You have a chronic behavior problem. Nothing seems to work.

Every now and then, we, as teachers, will have that behavior problem child in the class who resists all techniques aimed at correcting his or her actions.

Many of you are in teaching assignments where there is no outside help, no in-school support mechanisms, no counselors of any sort and, for various reasons, you can't or are not allowed to send that behavior problem student to the office or to a report room. You are left to deal with this disturbing student on your own.

Solution: One of the best assets you may have as far as behavior control is the mother, father, other relative or guardian of that child, if they are available.

Tell the student that due to his or her behavior, you find it necessary to invite his or her mother, father, other relative or guardian to the class to sit beside him or her.

The adult's role in your classroom is purely to help the student improve his or her attention skills and to therefore become a better learner.

In order to help the parent or guardian see how his or her child is behaving, have him or her fill in the Student Observation Chart (Figure 1–8). The behaviors to be observed are those that either add to learning skills or detract from them.

At the end of the school day or specified time period, you then have a meeting with the parent or guardian and the child to discuss the behaviors observed and those not observed this time.

Very often the mention of this idea is enough to shock the student into proper behavior. Students usually have an abhorrence to their parent or guardian attending school in this capacity.

In our society, there are many single parents or two-parent families who work. While they probably would like to come to the school during class times, it is impossible for them to do so. It is, therefore, important for you to make yourself aware of a student's family circumstance before you send the invitation.

You will find that your behavior problem child quite often will correct his or her own actions as a result of this idea and you will have a better liaison with that parent should other problems arise.

An added feature of this idea is the fact that it will have a moderating effect on the other students in the class. Word will soon get around that you don't fool around in Mrs. Jones's class because "she will call in your mom."

(Figure 1–8)

STUDENT OBSERVATION CHART

Behaviors to watch for	Put a check (✓) mark for each time behavior is observed	How many other students were involved? What did they do?
Student is talking at inappropriate times		
Student is out of desk, drops objects, throws something		
Student is daydreaming		
Student is not attentive to lesson		

13. QUICK RESPONSE FORMS—ONE AND TWO

Problem: Some students need parenting even while at school; they will not work unless they are continually under some sort of deadline or time pressure.

In our culture, many students do not have the family support to make them do the school work. The school system, therefore, must do what it can to take on that role and cause children to develop their potential at school. Even the brightest student will do poorly in school if there is no motivation.

How do you give much needed support to a student who has little or none at home? Which reporting form design is "user friendly" for the teacher and does not require a lot of teacher time to fill in, yet at the same time will keep your targeted student on task in all classes?

How can you show a student who has few people concerned about him or her that you actually care?

Solution 1: Use the Quick Response Form—One (Figure 1–9). This form asks three basic questions regarding the student's performance in the classes he or she attends. Question number one asks if the student was on task that particular day. The second question asks about the degree of diligence the student exhibited, and the third question asks if the student showed the teacher the actual school work.

(Figure 1–9)

QUICK RESPONSE FORM—ONE

Student: _____   Teacher: _____   Date: _____

Please rate this student's performance in class by placing a check (✓) mark in the appropriate space.

Subject	Was this student on task today?		Was this student working to the extent of capability?		Did this student show you any work?	
	YES	NO	YES	NO	YES	NO

The program the Quick Response Form represents is to be set up through a one-to-one conference with the student and the guiding or homeroom teacher.

Expectations and consequences should be laid out by the guiding teacher at this conference. Normally the student would carry a set of the Quick Response forms in a binder from class to class. The participating teachers would be given the binder at the end of each class, so it could be filled in. Only one form is used per day.

When a subject teacher gets the form from the student, that teacher need only make a check mark in the appropriate space; no detailed explanations are needed. If a subject teacher would like to add more details, then he or she is requested to write the necessary data on the reverse or back side of the form. That subject teacher may even want to call a meeting of the other teachers working with the student. Maximum communication is always a benefit for the child.

The student is told that he or she must report with the form to the supervising or homeroom teacher at the close of each school day. If any discussion is needed, it will occur at that time.

Solution #2: Use the second Quick Response form (Figure 1–10). This form requires the teacher to give a numerical rating of the student's performance on a particular day.

(Figure 1–10)

QUICK RESPONSE FORM—TWO

Date: _____

Student: _____   Teacher: _____

Please rate this student's performance in class by circling the appropriate performance on a scale of 1 to 5. <u>1 is poor and 5 is excellent</u>. Please include today's total score for this student.

SUBJECT	ON-TASK ABILITY	DID STUDENT WORK UP TO POTENTIAL?	BEHAVIOR IN CLASS	TOTAL
	1 2 3 4 5	1 2 3 4 5	1 2 3 4 5	
	1 2 3 4 5	1 2 3 4 5	1 2 3 4 5	
	1 2 3 4 5	1 2 3 4 5	1 2 3 4 5	
	1 2 3 4 5	1 2 3 4 5	1 2 3 4 5	
	1 2 3 4 5	1 2 3 4 5	1 2 3 4 5	
	1 2 3 4 5	1 2 3 4 5	1 2 3 4 5	
	1 2 3 4 5	1 2 3 4 5	1 2 3 4 5	
	1 2 3 4 5	1 2 3 4 5	1 2 3 4 5	
	1 2 3 4 5	1 2 3 4 5	1 2 3 4 5	
	1 2 3 4 5	1 2 3 4 5	1 2 3 4 5	
	1 2 3 4 5	1 2 3 4 5	1 2 3 4 5	
	1 2 3 4 5	1 2 3 4 5	1 2 3 4 5	
	1 2 3 4 5	1 2 3 4 5	1 2 3 4 5	

This form would normally be carried by the student in a binder from class to class. The student would give the form to the teacher after class. The teacher circles the appropriate number in each category as it relates to the behavior and on-task ability of the student. At the end of each school day, the student is to report to the homeroom or supervising teacher to discuss the ratings the various teachers gave him or her.

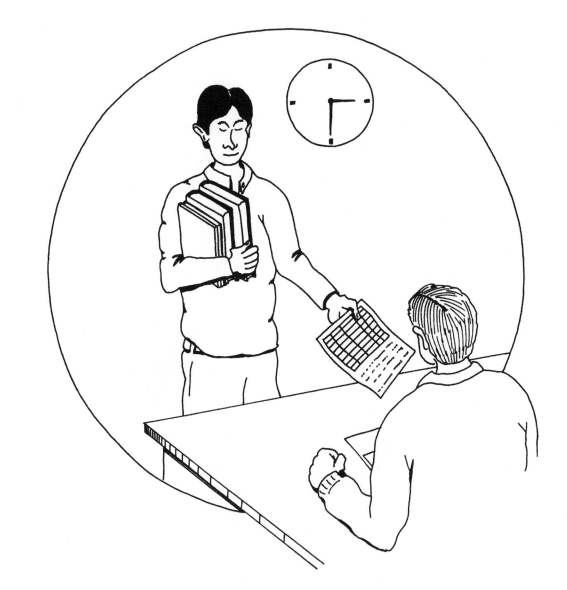

14. CHECK MARK TO PROGRESS

Problem: You want to promote positive behavior in your grade two class. You want students to understand from day one of school that you are trying to create a positive learning environment. This environment will only be developed in and through their interactions. How can you cause children to want to seek out proper behaviors?

Solution: Use the Check Mark to Progress program. This is a simple but effective method of identifying and rewarding those behaviors that lead to a happy, well-run classroom.

   The program proceeds as follows. When students are ready to begin on time, they receive a ✓ (check mark) beside their name. When students are polite, they receive a ✓ beside their name. When students render a service, they receive a ✓ beside their name. After a week, month or other time span, a Responsibility Certificate is given to those with the most check marks.

15. INTERIM REPORT IDEAS

Problem: It is a long time between report cards. You would like to keep the parents of your students informed about the academic and social skills development of their children between report cards.

What is the best way to make parents continually aware of the child's progress or lack of it?

Solution: Send out an interim report memo (Figures 1–11 and 1–12). This report focuses on a number of specific social and academic areas. A function of this report is a series of recommendations the students are asked to adhere to.

Each memo allows for teacher comments and parental feedback, thus facilitating open two-way communication.

The interim report card will have the effect of keeping students on their toes, if they know you are sending progress updates to their parents frequently.

Communication of this nature can really help to quell any criticisms that tend to arise when parents are not informed regularly about their child's progress.

Please note that this interim report memo is not designed to take the place of the report card. There is no place, other than the area for teacher comments, where student's marks are to be placed. Marks or grade scores should normally be left for the actual report card. It may become necessary, however, in certain circumstances, to include the grade marks for a child on this interim report memo.

Some jurisdictions may desire to use the interim report memo or progress report as an ongoing report card that is sent home every three or four weeks. This would be most effective at the primary grade levels and, in that case, grade scores would become part of the report.

(Figure 1–11)

INTERIM ATTITUDE/ACHIEVEMENT REPORT

MOM/DAD:

My teacher _____ wants to tell you what my attitude and achievements have been.

	VERY GOOD	GOOD	IMPROVING	NEEDS IMPROVING
ATTITUDE				
ACHIEVEMENT				

Recommendations (Plans for the future):

_____ Keep up the good work

_____ Must pay more attention in class

_____ Homework is to be completed regularly

_____ Overall effort and attitude must improve

_____ Student must be better prepared for class (pens, pencils, paper, etc.)

_____ Parent-Teacher Conference required

Teacher Comments:	Parent Comments:
_____	_____
_____	_____
_____	_____
_____	_____
_____	_____
_____	_____
_____	_____
Teacher Signature _____	Parent Signature _____

(Figure 1–12)

INTERIM PROGRESS REPORT

Name: _____   Date: _____

Class: _____   Teacher: _____

Subject: _____   Guidance Counselor: _____

E (Excellent),   G (Good),   F (Fair),   P (Poor)

_____ degree of motivation   _____ grade scores

_____ working to potential   _____ attitude toward homework

_____ attendance   _____ pays attention in class

_____ punctuality to school   _____ participates in class discussion

_____ punctuality to class   _____ relates well to others

_____ attitude to studies   _____ brings materials to class

Plans for the future (recommendations):

_____ continue the good work   _____ more serious approach to studies

_____ Parent/Teacher Conference required   _____ student should be better prepared

_____ homework needs to be completed _____ student will seek after-school help

_____ classwork is to improve   _____ student will improve behavior

Additional Comments: _____

_____

_____

Parental Comments: _____

_____

_____

16. IN-CLASS STUDY PERIODS

Problem: You find that student marks on your tests and quizzes are low. You suspect and, in many cases, know, students are not studying at home. You realize that some student home situations are not conducive to studying.

How do you make sure students study your material for the tests you give?

Solution: Have an in-class study period just prior to the test. With this period you can control the studying process and are available to answer any questions that might arise.

You tell the students in the in-class study period there is to be no talking and no studying together in pairs or groups as this leads mainly to visiting instead of actual studying.

During the in-class study, you have the option to review data or to reinforce a point or two.

The in-class study assures you that all students present have had the opportunity to cover the necessary data.

Students will come to expect an in-class study period before your tests and will save questions for that time. Parents will appreciate this because it indicates to them that you are making a conscientious effort to make the students internalize the data.

I include the in-class study sign (Figure 1–13). It is best to place one copy in front of the students taped to the blackboard and one copy on the outside part of the door to let all know that the in-class study period is in progress.

© 1996 by The Center for Applied Research in Education

(Figure 1–13)

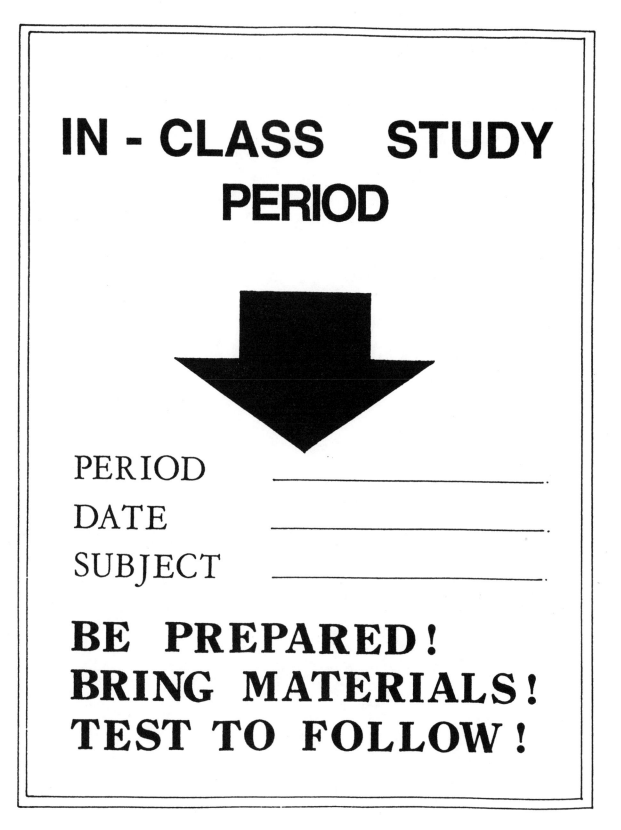

17. OUT-OF-THE-ROOM CONTROL BOARD

Problem: In your large class of students, you are in a situation of crowd control, behavior management and finally, some teaching. In this environment, you are the center of a barrage of requests, demands, and so forth. It is not always easy to keep track of which student or students are at the washroom or out of the room for some other reason.

It may be essential to control which students are out of the room simultaneously. You may find it necessary to implement a policy of not having two students of the same gender at the washroom at the same time. What is an easy way to monitor how many and which students are at the washroom or out of the room at any given point in the school day?

Solution #1: Make an Out-of-the-Room Control Board, Style 1. This is a large piece of cardboard on which you glue three durable pockets. One pocket is the "in" pocket and the other two are the "out" pockets; one for girls and one for boys.

On suitable sized cards, write the name of each student in bold letters with a marking pen. Once all the cards are made, store them in the "in" pocket. You then need to instruct the students that when they leave the room, they are to take their card from the "in" pocket and place it in the appropriate "out" pocket.

During the ongoing busy day of the classroom, you can see at a glance which and how many students are out of the room.

Solution #2: The Out-of-the-Room Control Board, Style 2. Place each student's name on a card. Glue the cards onto a board or better still, tape or glue them onto a piece of suitable sized pegboard.

The girls' names are to be in one row and the boys' names above or below in a separate row. Place a hook below each student's name. At the start of each of the two rows, have a separate hook with a sign that says "out" or "boy out" or "girl out."

When a student asks to go to the washroom, he or she will take the "out" sign and hang it on the hook below his or her name. This monitor system will inform you and the students instantly who is out of the classroom.

If a particular student frequently has the "out" sign under his or her name, this will give you an awareness that something must be done to help the child in this area.

For both styles of the Out-of-the-Room Control Board, there should be a discretionary factor built into this. Students should be told that in the case of a genuine emergency, that the washroom is available to them even if someone of the same gender is at the facility.

© 1996 by The Center for Applied Research in Education

18. THE ASSIGNMENT TRACKING CHART

Problem: Parents have received "the" report card. They find that their son Johnny has neglected to do a major portion of his assignments. The parent phones you, the homeroom teacher, to ask why she was not informed earlier of her son's tardiness. You, as the homeroom teacher, only teach Johnny one subject so you had no idea he was late with assignments in his other classes.

How do you help parents keep track of a student's assignment performance in the classes you do not teach?

Solution: Use the Assignment Tracking Chart (Figure 1–14). This chart is given to the student by the supervising teacher once a week (usually Friday). The student carries it to each teacher he or she is taught by. The teachers, upon receiving the chart, will write in any assignments that are due or indicate any tests that are in the offing.

The chart is carried by the student to his or her parents and then back to the homeroom or monitoring teacher the next school day.

You will note that there is a space for the parents to sign the chart before it is returned to the teacher. This helps ensure that the parents are informed of upcoming assignments or tests.

(Figure 1–14)

ASSIGNMENT TRACKING CHART

Date: _____

_____ needs to complete all assignments this term.
        (Student Name)

Please indicate if this student owes you an assignment or has a test to study for.

Teacher's Name	Type of Assignment or Test to Study For	Due Date or Date of Test

_____
                  Parent's Signature

RETURN TO MONITORING TEACHER THE NEXT SCHOOL DAY

19. CONTRACTS

Problem: Many students need a formalized direction process. In other words, they need a plan of action or an agreement on paper to keep them on course.

Solution: Use contracts (Figure 1–15) with the students. The contract is basically an agreement between the teacher or school official and the student. It is a statement that an agreed-to set of behaviors will be adhered to and an agreed-to set of tasks will be completed.

The contract form should state exactly what work the student will perform and under what conditions the contract is valid. The more concrete the language of the contract, the better it will be understood by the parties. The teacher should avoid vague terms and nebulous concepts. Language should be concise.

The success of any contract at the school level is a direct function of two factors:

a)   The student needs to have a mature concept of what a contract is and what it is supposed to do.

b)   The greater the consistency and reliability of the teacher/supervisor administering the contract the better will be the results.

In extreme cases where there ends up being litigation as a result of a student's errant behavior, the evidence of the contract is very important. It will show the courts in a succinct way that the teacher and school system were on task in terms of behavior correction.

© 1996 by The Center for Applied Research in Education

(Figure 1–15)

CONTRACT

THIS IS TO CERTIFY THAT _____

WILL PERFORM THE FOLLOWING: _____

_____

_____

CONDITIONS OF CONTRACT:

_____

_____

STUDENT: _____

TEACHER: _____

DATE: _____

20. SPEAK SOFTLY BECAUSE YOU CAN'T CARRY A STICK ANY MORE

Problem: You walk into a classroom and there is a loud chatter going on. How do you quiet down the students without stressfully shouting your brains out?

Solution: With this idea I am taking a page from the old adage "Speak softly but carry a big stick," except that I'm leaving out the stick part.

Stand directly in front of the class and begin speaking in a low soft tone of voice somewhat above a whisper.

First one student will notice you are saying something, then several others will see this happening. What occurs most often is that one of those students will tell the others to be quiet.

The nice thing about this idea is that it allows you to control the class and conversation with a minimum of expended energy.

This is especially effective in the upper grades and at seminars where there is a greater level of maturity in the audience.

21. FOCUS POINT OF ORDER AND Q

Problem: There are times when you enter a class and the students will just not settle down. How do you control the class quickly when the usual techniques do not work?

Solution 1: In order to bring the class under control, you go to the blackboard and write the word "Focus" and directly beside the word you write a time that is near the end of that particular period. If, for example, the period ends at 3:30 P.M., you write 3:25 P.M. on the board beside the word "Focus." You then tell the students that we must focus on that time. You are going to give everyone in the class five minutes at the end to fulfil their "talking needs." Everyone, however, must work now in order to get the reward of the five minutes at the end of the period.

You then appoint the most talkative member of the class to be the time monitor. That student is to tell you when it is 3:25 P.M. so you can give the class the five minutes of "talking needs" fulfillment.

This technique works well for you because to give up five minutes at the end is easily worth having the students work diligently during the first part of the period.

Solution #2: The first letter in the word quiet is Q. This is perhaps one of the most unique letters of the alphabet. When you want to settle a class down quickly and with no stress to yourself, go to the blackboard and slowly write the letter Q. Then put a box around the Q. Due to their innate sense of curiosity, all students will now focus on your strange behavior. Likewise, students know, consciously or unconsciously, that Q relates to being quiet. Therefore, they will all concentrate on your little box with the letter Q in it. Now that you have their attention, you can begin to teach the class.

22. GEOMETRY SET CONTROL

Problem: Geometry sets can be a source of troubles. Those troubles range from the loss of the set to the puncture of an eyeball from an errant compass.

How can you minimize the danger potential of school geometry sets as well as control the lost or stolen geometry set problem?

Solution: Gather all the students' geometry sets at the beginning of each year. Label each set with the appropriate student's name.

When you come to the unit on geometry in February, you give out the parts of the geometry set that each individual needs. It is important that you do not give the complete sets back to the students unless absolutely necessary. Normally students work on only one part of geometric studies at a time. If they are measuring angles in the text, they need a protractor. They do not need a compass. Give out only what is needed. This will prevent loss of those parts that are not being used. The compass is the device to watch out for. There has been many a punctured body part because of this instrument and rigid control is absolutely necessary.

At the end of each lesson, you can gather up the geometry set parts for safe keeping.

When school is finished for the year, ask the students if they want their geometry sets back or if they want to donate them. You then add these donated sets to your collection.

Controlling the problems associated with the geometry set is important because the contents are necessary for much of the work in any geometry unit. If a student loses his or her set, it often leaves the teacher with a frustrated scramble to provide a protractor or two.

23. HAVE A NOTE PAPER SUPPLY

Problem: A major source of trouble for many teachers is the substance you are looking at right now—paper.

There are those students who will continually not bring note paper to class. Whether intentional or otherwise, many students will show up at class without anything to write on. This of course will result in you having to send the student to his or her locker to get the necessary paper. As you know this causes the student to miss the data you presented while he or she was out and it creates 'x' amount of disturbance as the student reenters the class. How do you avoid the note paper hassle in a way that serves you and the student most efficiently?

Solution: Give the students a sheet or two of note paper when you feel it is necessary. However, before you say, "No way am I supplying the students with paper," please read on.

The looseleaf supply is kept at your desk and must be used sparingly upon your discretion. It is only there to solve *your* problems, not to be a continuous source of writing paper for the students.

A good source of this note paper can come at the end of the school year. A call for donations at this time may net you enough note paper to make it through the following school year.

24. THE IN-CLASS AUCTION

Problem: You are incredibly busy in your regular classroom and there seems to be an increasing demand on your time and circumstance. You are looking for a unique behavior control program that works. You need an idea that has its own momentum, or is self-policing. In other words, you want the students to help control their own behavior. What behavior modification system can you set up or implement that will help the students target positive behaviors and thereby relieve some of your pressures?

Solution: Develop the In-Class Auction. With this idea, you auction off items or privileges that are of value to the students. The wearing of a hat during class time is a good example. This auction usually takes place at the end of each month or term or whenever you feel the time is right.

With this idea, students must have some kind of tender to bid with, so you allow the students to earn tokens. These tokens are color coded for your records. The green tokens are the ones the students bid with. The red tokens take away or destroy green tokens, so the reds must be avoided at all cost.

The idea here is to key the earning of green tokens to positive behavior and the earning or gaining of red tokens to negative behavior.

How you value the greens and the reds is up to you. Most teachers would subtract the reds from the greens on a one-to-one basis. This may vary from class to class.

It is necessary with this type of auction system to keep good records. A large binder placed on the desk is usually sufficient as a recordkeeping log book. The In-Class Auction Record Sheet (Figure 1–16) is provided to help you in this area.

(Figure 1–16)

IN-CLASS AUCTION RECORD SHEET

MONTH OF _____

NAME	GREEN TOKENS (POSITIVE VALUE)	RED TOKENS (NEGATIVE VALUE)	TOTAL

25. HELP FOR THE DISTRACTED STUDENT

Problem: Betty and Bobby cannot keep on track. They seem to be distracted. The least little stimulus is enough to send their minds out to left field.

What is a quick, cheap and effective way to keep easily distracted students on task?

Solution: Once you have identified the child who is quickly off task, remove that person from his or her surroundings (peers) and place that student in the midst of excellent working students. Surround that child with quality workers on all four sides. If possible, have those good workers two or three deep around the targeted student.

The easily distracted student should also be as far as possible from other stimuli, such as fish tanks, classroom windows or open doors. You will immediately notice the student in question will have more of a task orientation, as well as improved performance on those tasks. The better workers will not be less on task because of the easily distracted student in their midst. They will keep up their high quality of work.

In essence, the peers around the easily off-task student will set the standard for him or her to follow.

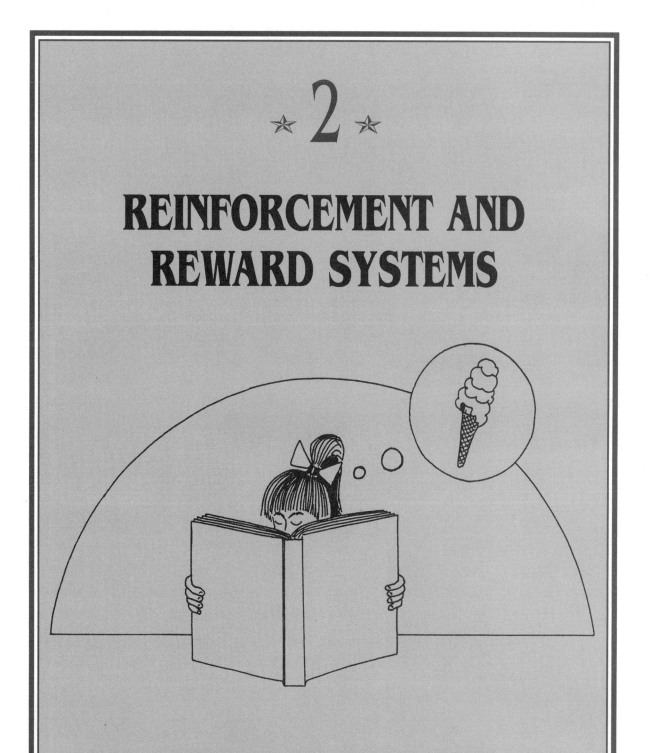

✫ 2 ✫

REINFORCEMENT AND REWARD SYSTEMS

Students will perform at peak efficiency if they know there is a meaningful and tangible reward for them to attain. The rewards do not need to be high cost in terms of money or energy.

Included in this section are not only individual rewards, but we also develop whole-school and grade-level reinforcement systems. These are described through really great innovative ideas that have passed the test of time.

26. PERCENT TICKETS

Problem: You need an instant reward system for work well done or for the completion of special tasks.

Solution: Offer percent tickets as rewards (Figure 2–1). A percent ticket is a document that is worth percentage points for tests, essays or reports.

If a student performs extra well in math or does some special work for you, you then give the student a ticket worth anywhere from 1% to 5%. The student can use the ticket to raise any grade on tests, reports and essays, and so forth, in any of the subjects you teach that student. It may be convenient for you to limit percent tickets to the subject area in which it was earned; this is at your discretion.

Under normal circumstances, if Betty obtains a score of 90% on a test and she turns in to you 4% worth of percent tickets, her mark for the test would be recorded as 94%.

Percent tickets are not to be used liberally as other rewards are because there can be too much of a good thing here. The school grade may become skewed and not reflect the students' real academic ability. The ticket, therefore, should only be used to upgrade a particular test, report or essay mark and not to upgrade the whole term mark. I destroy a percent ticket once it has been redeemed.

I allow percent tickets to be kept from one term to the next but not from year to year.

Students should be told that the percent ticket they get from you is only good with you and cannot be redeemed by Mr. Jones down the hall who teaches history.

(Figure 2–1)

PERCENT TICKET

The Value Of This Ticket Is _____ %.

Redeem this to upgrade any test, report or

essay assigned in _____ *class this school*
(teacher's name)

year.

_____
STUDENT'S NAME

_____
DATE

_____
TEACHER'S INITIALS

27. SPECIAL PRIVILEGES PASS CARD

Problem: How do the teachers and school administrators create a positive behavior attitude in the school? How do you make students want to have respect for themselves and others as well as for the physical school itself? How can the staff maintain meaningful rewards for good behavior over the entire length of the school year?

Solution: Introduce a positive behavior pass card system. The pass cards are to be given to students who have a record of excellent behavior. The pass card allows the owner to have special privileges around the school such as early entry into the school, access to areas such as the computer room or the gym, if supervision is available.

The pass cards (Figure 2–3) must be applied for and are only given to those students who have demonstrated that they deserve them. The criteria upon which the teaching staff bases the giving out of the cards is purely subjective. These criteria must be keyed to your particular school environment as are the rewards and privileges associated with card ownership.

When a student applies for a card, every teacher (or other staff) who knows the child will review the application (Figure 2–2). If one teacher rejects an applicant, then the pass card is not given to the student. This makes the pass card a thing of value because there is a process the student must go through to obtain it and not all students will possess it. It becomes a goal to strive for and therefore the behaviors needed to obtain it will become a goal to strive for.

(Figure 2–2)

APPLICATION FOR PASS CARD

NAME: _____   GRADE: _____

AGE: _____

DATE: _____   CLASSROOM: _____

TEACHER: _____

1.   Write several reasons why you should be given a pass card.

_____

_____

_____

_____

_____

2.   Which activities would you like to use a pass card for?

_____

_____

_____

_____   _____
STUDENT SIGNATURE   PARENT APPROVAL SIGNATURE

****

TEACHER	APPROVED	REJECTED	REASON FOR REJECTION

(Figure 2–3)

special privilege
PASS CARD

Name:_____ Gr____
Date of issue:_____
Principal's initials:_____

    * All school rules must be observed

special privilege
PASS CARD

Name:_____ Gr____
Date of issue:_____
Principal's initials:_____

    * All school rules must be observed

special privilege
PASS CARD

Name:_____ Gr____
Date of issue:_____
Principal's initials:_____

    * All school rules must be observed

special privilege
PASS CARD

Name:_____ Gr____
Date of issue:_____
Principal's initials:_____

    * All school rules must be observed

special privilege
PASS CARD

Name:_____ Gr____
Date of issue:_____
Principal's initials:_____

    * All school rules must be observed

special privilege
PASS CARD

Name:_____ Gr____
Date of issue:_____
Principal's initials:_____

    * All school rules must be observed

28. FREEBIE DAY

Problem: Are there any management ideas that apply to the whole school, complete class or grade level? Are there any ideas that will bolster morale, stimulate performance and reinforce positive behavior?

Solution: Develop a "Freebie Day" at the end of each month. This is the day in which an event or activity (dance, video games, and so forth) is planned to occur during school hours.

Students who have successfully fulfilled a stated set of criteria are given a ticket to attend Freebie Day while those who have not met the criteria are required to remain at the regular classroom to complete their tasks.

The criteria to be fulfilled for the average Freebie Day could include:

a) Students must complete all homework assignments to the teacher's satisfaction for that month.

b) Students must have a record of good, respectful and reasonable behavior.

c) There must be no lates or unexplained absences on the part of the student for that month.

You will notice that some of these criteria are objective (following a set of rules) while others are subjective, giving you, the teaching staff, the discretionary powers with which to make the final decision on who gets to go to Freebie Day and who does not.

It is best to advertise this program and its month-end rewards about one to two weeks before the event, thus generating interest and thereby stimulating positive behavior in the area of your stated criteria.

Figure 2–4 is an example of the type of poster than can be used to promote Freebie Day.

© 1996 by The Center for Applied Research in Education

(Figure 2–4)

FREEBIE DAY FOR
GRADE 8'S AND 9'S !!!!!!!!!

HERE'S HOW TO EARN YOUR TICKET TO FREEBIE DAY **FOR THE MONTH OF** OCTOBER .

DURING THE FIRST WEEK OF NOVEMBER AN ACTIVITY WILL BE HELD DURING SCHOOL HOURS. YOU WILL BE ABLE TO LEAVE YOUR CLASSES TO ATTEND IF:

1) YOU HAVE COMPLETED ALL OF YOUR HOMEWORK ASSIGNMENTS TO YOUR TEACHER'S SATISFACTION IN THE MONTH OF <u>OCTOBER</u>, AND ...

2) YOU HAVE BEHAVED REASONABLY, RESPONSIBLY, AND RESPECTABLY BOTH IN AND OUT OF CLASS IN THE MONTH OF <u>OCTOBER</u>, AND ...

3) YOU HAVE NO LATES IN THE MONTH OF <u>OCTOBER</u>, AND ...

4) YOU HAVE NO UNEXPLAINED ABSENCES FOR THE MONTH OF <u>OCTOBER</u>

HOPE TO SEE YOU THERE!!!!!!!!

29. NO-COST OR LOW-COST REWARDS FOR STUDENTS

Problem: Most teachers are in the "continuous reinforcement for positive behavior" business. In order to facilitate that reinforcement, teachers need meaningful rewards. The trouble is the rewards can be costly. If you purchase rewards, you will find yourself paying for your students' education. Where do you access no-cost or low-cost rewards for students?

Solution: Review this list of fifty rewards that can be developed with and in the classroom or school. These rewards for the most part take advantage of the ongoing processes of the school.

50 No-Cost or Low-Cost Rewards for Students:

1. Allow students to have early entrance into the school.
2. Provide extra time in the computer lab.
3. Provide access to the telephone.
4. Have a games period or time. Students bring their own games.
5. Rent or buy cartoons for the video machine.
6. Make it a privilege to raise or lower the flag.
7. Offer opportunities to work in the hall outside your classroom.
8. Make a "pick a treat box" containing erasers, pencils, sports cards, and so forth.
9. Ask a fast-food chain to donate hamburger or french fry vouchers to be used as rewards.
10. Allow students who are good to not have to do a question or two.
11. Provide a period or half period off from school work.
12. Play music for the students; a favorite tape or turning the radio on works well here.
13. Invite an amateur magician or ventriloquist to perform in class.
14. Arrange for excellent work of students to appear in the newspaper.
15. Arrange for the picture of students to appear in the newspaper to highlight an event or behavior.
16. Bring a movie for the students to watch.
17. Allow for a day or period when students can eat junk food in class.
18. Walk to an ice cream parlor—students buy.
19. Have a free art period—students can draw anything they want.
20. Ask a parent to bake a cake or make some cookies.
21. Let a student work with the janitor or secretary for period of time.
22. Have a class party.
23. Have a gym night at the school for students and parents.
24. Allow students to read teen magazines, comic books or car magazines.

25. Take the students outside for baseball, broomball, and so forth.
26. Put colorful stick-on stars on the student's work.
27. Paint the faces of the students one day (younger grades, of course).
28. Ask the local soft drink company to donate a case or two. They usually have part of their P.R. budget set aside for this.
29. Provide a video games period when students bring hand-held or T.V.-use video games.
30. Have a non-pointy paper airplane-making contest.
31. Let a student teach a class.
32. Read a story to the students.
33. Take students on a field trip—to a zoo or museum, for example.
34. Let a student clean the brushes.
35. Let students decorate the bulletin board.
36. Invite a guest speaker.
37. Allow a student to run errands for you.
38. Do stylized name art. Write each student's name on art paper; they then color it in.
39. Extend recess.
40. Provide word puzzles and crossword puzzles for the students.
41. Organize a fun fair games day.
42. Offer free tickets to school sporting events.
43. Ask someone to come in to play a musical instrument.
44. Let students chew gum. Have a bubble gum blowing contest.
45. Give out "free from homework tickets"—good for one time free from homework.
46. Allow students to choose the sport at the gym.
47. Switch a class from English to Art.
48. Put jelly beans in a jar for every good thing. When you collect enough share them with the class (watch for diabetics).
49. Stickers, especially scratch-and-sniff ones, are a good reward for the younger set.
50. Start a term awards program.

30. GOOD GUY, GOOD GIRL AND CONGRATULATIONS AWARDS

Problem: Students like concrete rewards. They need direct, positive reinforcement for a job well done. Students need to know their parents know that their teacher thinks highly of them. What types of rewards can you give to students that are low cost, meaningful, concrete and can be shown to parents and/or relatives?

Solution: Give out Good Guy and Good Girl and Congratulations Awards (Figure 2–5, 2-6 and 2-7). These are awards that can be either directly given to the student or mailed home.

Whenever a student does a good deed in your estimation or you feel a student needs a special lift or reward, the Good Guy or Good Girl Award is ideal.

Children with good behavior patterns don't get much attention from teachers because they can function quite well on their own. They, too often, are not encouraged because we feel they have the confidence in their intellectual capacity. This confidence may not be there, however. When the good do good we should encourage them all the more with the Good Guy, Good Girl or Congratulations Award.

This type of award remains significant to the student for many years.

One note of caution here. Like all awards, they should be used sparingly and only when there is a genuine cause to give them out. Otherwise, the awards will be meaningless if most students receive them frequently.

© 1996 by The Center for Applied Research in Education

GOOD BOY AWARD

GOOD GIRL AWARD

(Figure 2–7)

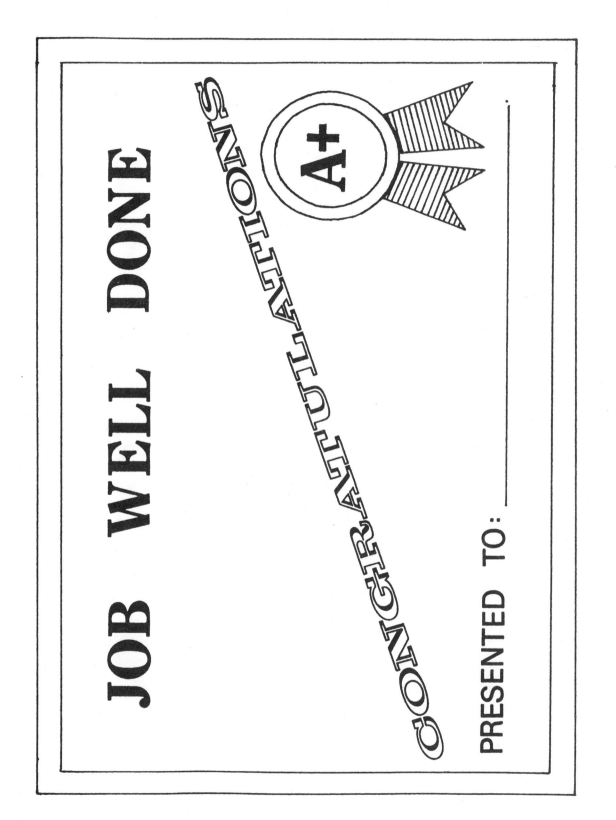

31. THE READING TICKET PROGRAM

Problem: You need a reading incentive program that will help the students to become successful readers. You would like the parents to know that their child is actively strengthening his or her reading skills in your program. What kind of school-home project will cause students to want to read?

Solution: Use the Reading Ticket program (Figure 2–8). Each student is given either a five-pack or a ten-pack of reading tickets to take home with the reading book they have signed out from the library. Students are to read their books for fifteen- or thirty-minute units of time. When the student finishes one time unit, he or she fills in and then takes the ticket to his or her parents for a signature. This instantly makes the parents aware of your progressive reading program and of the amount of time their child is spending reading each day.

The reading ticket has two parts—a right side and a left side. When the ticket or tickets are returned to your class, you fill in, then tear off the left side and place this in a draw drum or barrel. At the end of each month, a draw is made from the barrel and the winner receives a prize provided by you or by some supporting business or service club in your area.

It doesn't take students very long to figure out that the more they read, the more stubs they will have in the draw drum and the more likely they are to win a prize.

The right side of the reading ticket is hung on display under each child's name on your bulletin board. Parents, visiting your class, can see at a glance the total amount of reading their child has accomplished.

There are some children whose home circumstance is not conducive to reading or even getting the ticket signed by someone. Due to these cases, it is a good idea to use the reading tickets for your regular classroom reading. This will allow those disadvantaged students some chance of having a ticket stub or two in the draw drum and therefore, a chance at winning a prize.

(Figure 2–8)

Name: _____ | **MY READING TICKET FOR** _____
Grade: _____ | (Date)
Date: _____ | STUDENT: _____

TITLE OF BOOK
OR ARTICLE: _____ _____
MINUTES READ

PARENT OR
TEACHER: _____
(SIGNATURE)

Name: _____ | **MY READING TICKET FOR** _____
Grade: _____ | (Date)
Date: _____ | STUDENT: _____

TITLE OF BOOK
OR ARTICLE: _____ _____
MINUTES READ

PARENT OR
TEACHER: _____
(SIGNATURE)

Name: _____ | **MY READING TICKET FOR** _____
Grade: _____ | (Date)
Date: _____ | STUDENT: _____

TITLE OF BOOK
OR ARTICLE: _____ _____
MINUTES READ

PARENT OR
TEACHER: _____
(SIGNATURE)

32. THE "GOTCHA" PROGRAM

Problem: We want to create a positive atmosphere in our school. We want to reward good behavior, increase self-esteem and reinforce fundamental values of the human spirit.

Solution: Institute the "Gotcha" program in your school. This is a reward program for positive behaviors seen around the school.

When a staff member sees any student doing something positive (picking up someone's fallen book for them) that staff member writes it on a note pad or piece of paper. The information is then given to the principal. The principal enters the student's name on a Gotcha Certificate (Figure 2–9). Every staff member including janitors, teacher aides, secretaries and teachers are included as part of the team. Any one of them can give out a "Gotcha" for good deeds they observe. When the whole staff is involved, it makes the students see each teacher, janitor, and so forth as a potential source of rewards for them. In this situation, staff-student relationships are strengthened.

When the students are gathered for the weekly assembly, the principal then gives out the certificates. It is best if the "Gotcha" certificates are given out with some gusto. For example: "Judy, we 'gotcha' for ..." The principal would then go on to describe in appropriate detail the good thing the student had accomplished.

The "Gotcha" program will have a ripple effect throughout the whole school. Students will be looking to help others as well as have a heightened awareness of what is a positive way to act and what is not.

A good way to bolster this idea is by including more tangible rewards. If you design an appropriate letter you can obtain donations of small prizes from the business community or you may be able to enlist the help of a local service club. They are quite often willing to donate prizes and even do some of the prize presentations.

The "Gotcha" program is unique in that it serves to justify the school's positive image while it makes doing good things a goal to be achieved.

(Figure 2–9)

"GOTCHA"

CERTIFICATE

This is to certify that

_____

performed a good deed on

_____ *19* __

as witnessed by _____

33. THE ICE CREAM READING IDEA

Problem: You need a neat incentive idea to stimulate reading by your grade two's. You plan to reward them by appealing to their taste buds.

Solution: Use the old ice cream scoop reading technique. Photocopy an ice cream cone and scoops (Figure 2–10) for each child. Place the cones on the bulletin board or wall in the classroom. Every time a child reads a book, you add a scoop of ice cream to the cone. Once everyone has reached your magic number of ice cream scoops (usually 4 or more), you then take the whole class out for an ice cream cone or you bring the ice cream and the cones to the classroom to treat the class.

It is best to have the scoops of ice cream and the cone in various bright colors. This will help make the students aware of their common goal of getting the excellent treat.

You will find that once you have treated the class to an ice cream reward, you will have little, if any, trouble getting the class to add scoops to their cones a second time—and if you are not counting calories, indulge!

(Figure 2–10)

34. PARTICIBUCKS

Problem: You have reluctant "joiners" in your school. It is difficult even during the best of times to get students to sign up for the volleyball team, debate team, and so forth.

You are looking for an effective positive reinforcement idea that will draw students into your sports or other extracurricular programs.

What type of reward system can you initiate that will cause students to want to participate in school activities?

Solution: Start the Particibucks program. With this idea, students are given X amount of particibucks for taking part in the various programs in your school (Figure 2–11).

This idea can and should be used for all extracurricular activities. With this in mind, the start-up rewards for each area could differ. This means that if you pay one hundred dollars in particibucks as a signing bonus for the football team that traditionally has a good turnout, you could pay three hundred fifty particibucks as a sign-up bonus for the volleyball team that desperately needs players.

In the sign-up situation, the bonuses should not be paid out until mid-season or even near the season end to avoid sign up "particiquitters."

Particibucks are earned as students perform well in each different event area. The distribution of the bucks would therefore have to be at the discretion of the coach or teacher supervisor.

The particibucks themselves are to be used by the students to purchase prizes or privileges that the teachers have collected or allowed to happen. It is best that the sale of these prizes and privileges be held once a month, so the whole school population can see concrete results of participating. It is important to display the prizes and list the privileges in the school trophy case. This provides effective free advertising for your incentive program.

The type and quality of rewards is up to the staff. A quick survey of the students will reveal what is currently of value in the teen culture. Rewards need not be expensive. An autographed picture of a teen idol would have the whole school buzzing (more free advertising) as would a signed football from a popular pro team. You will find that a few letters to the right fan club will bring many rewards. These people are often more than willing to help out educational programs.

It is best to individualize the particibucks. You do not want them to become transferable from student to student. If particibucks can be traded around the school, you will defeat your purpose. Students who did not participate will end up with some of the particibucks and therefore some of the prizes or privileges.

You will find that a program such as particibucks will have the effect of changing attitudes toward taking part in extracurricular programs. What may have been a school of reluctant joiners will soon become a school of enthusiastic participants.

(Figure 2–11)

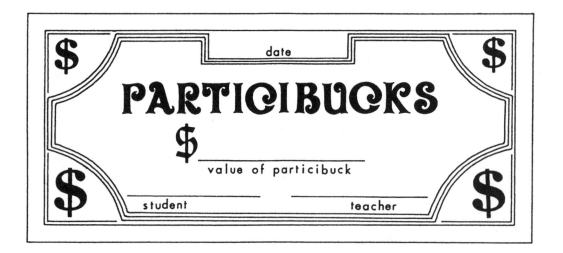

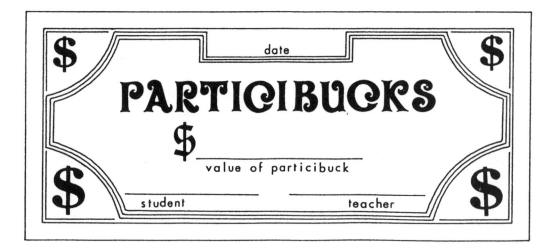

★ 3 ★

ON-TASK BEHAVIOR

This section on "On-Task Behavior" shows how to use innovative ideas to keep students working up to their ability.

As you know, students will learn at an accelerated pace if they can be made to focus on their work. Techniques to enrich this concentration are found in this section.

35. THE STICK JAR

Problem: You want to keep all students on their toes. This is perhaps the hardest task for all of us in the area of teaching. We want our audiences to pay attention to us one hundred percent of the time because we give a one hundred percent effort in our presentations.

How can we keep students' attention at a high level?

Solution: Use the attention-producing Stick Jar. This idea has two basic parts to it: an opaque glass jar and a number of wooden ice cream sticks or tongue depressors. You will need one stick for each person in the class or group you are instructing. Before you start your session, have students write their name on a stick. Place all the sticks vertically into the jar. Place the jar in a high profile location such as on your speaking podium or on your desk where all students or participants can clearly see it.

When you want a student to answer a question or perform a particular task, you draw a name from the stick jar. That person would have to answer the question or perform that important task you need to get done.

Your students are kept attentive because they never know when their name will be pulled from the jar. The stick jar is objective. One stick feels like another when you reach into the jar. No one can accuse you of favoring one student over another because all names have an equal opportunity to be pulled.

You, the teacher, can manipulate the jar if you so desire by marking the top edge of certain sticks if you want to focus on a particular student. You may feel it is necessary to leave a student's name out of the jar all together. This is at your discretion.

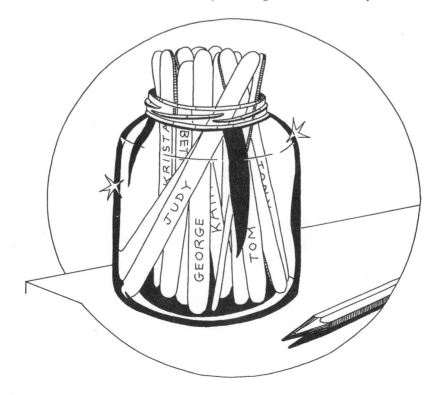

36. GRADE STANDING CHART

Problem: Many times a student will be unaware of his or her standing in a particular class. Students will forget their score on the last test or essay and, therefore, will only have a vague idea of how well they are performing.

It is safe to assume that if a student does not know exactly where he or she stands, then it is more likely than not that the parents of that student do not know either.

How do you keep a consciousness in the students' mind of their current grade performance in your class? What tool can be used to instantly inform parents of the grade standing of their child?

Solution: In order to keep the students constantly aware of their grade status in your class, it is an excellent idea to use the Current Grade Standing Chart (Figure 3–1).

This chart lists the scores and other results from tests, quizzes and essays that the student has been evaluated on during the term or whole year.

When a student receives a grade on a test, he or she would immediately write that score on the "Current Grade Standing Chart."

This chart gives the student an exact idea of where he or she stands in relation to your subject. It gives the student a frame of reference. He or she has a constant reminder of which areas need improvement.

This chart will help the parents understand what their child's status is in terms of a particular class or classes. Once the parents are made aware of the existence of the chart, they need only look at their child's binder to have an update of their child's performance.

(Figure 3–1)

CURRENT GRADE STANDING CHART

SUBJECT		1	2	3	4	5	6	7	8	9
	TEST DATE									
	TEST SCORE									
	TEST DATE									
	TEST SCORE									
	TEST DATE									
	TEST SCORE									
	TEST DATE									
	TEST SCORE									
	TEST DATE									
	TEST SCORE									
	TEST DATE									
	TEST SCORE									
	TEST DATE									
	TEST SCORE									

37. PRORATING A TEST

Problem: You are searching for that nirvana of teaching circumstances—the "fair" test. You want a test that will evaluate the exact skill level you are targeting as well as give the students some choice in the evaluation process. You want a test or quiz that in itself is a learning tool or a decision-making device.

Solution: Develop the prorated test. This test forces the student to make a decision as to how many and which questions he or she will do in a test.

The prorated test is structured as follows:

In a math test of twenty questions, for example, students must answer the first ten questions of the twenty. The other questions from eleven to twenty are optional. Students are allowed to do any of the questions from eleven to twenty. They do not necessarily have to be done in chronological order. Those students who stop after answering ten questions will then be graded on ten. These students should be made aware that for each wrong answer, ten points or ten percent will be removed from their total score. Through this, students should understand that the more questions they answer, the less costly the error; however, the more questions the student answers, the greater the likelihood of making a mistake. This is the key reason the prorated test is an excellent decision-making tool. Students must assess the remaining questions, after they have answered the required number, to see if indeed it is of value for them to answer any more.

This test will be perceived as more equitable or "fair" because the students actually have some choice in the structure of the evaluation. This type of test or quiz will cut down the amount of after-test blues often associated with difficult tests.

© 1996 by The Center for Applied Research in Education

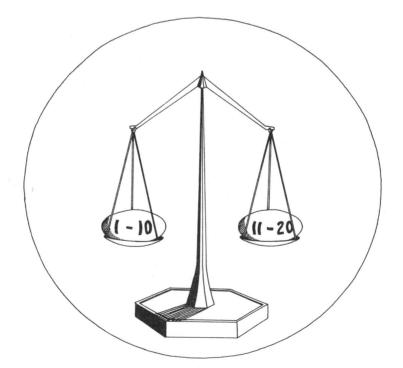

38. GUIDELINES AND JUDGING FORM FOR SCHOOL ORATORY COMPETITIONS

Problem: In many schools, there is, or should be, a school oratory or public speaking competition. In a culture where communication skills are becoming increasingly important, it is necessary to promote public speaking as a skill vital to the students' future.

Which set of rules or ideas would help the teacher set up an oratory program? What is an effective tool that could examine a useful set of criteria for judging an oratory competition?

Solution: Introduce the following set of student guidelines or rules that are needed to develop an effective oratory or public speaking competition. These guidelines cultivate the skill areas that are necessary at the high school and junior high school levels.

These skills areas are listed on the evaluation tool (Figure 3-2) that the judges will use.

Guidelines:

1. Students are asked to prepare their speech on a topic of their choice. Their topic choice is to be submitted to the teacher/supervisors for approval.

2. Students are asked to write their speech on 3 × 5 index cards.

3. Index cards are for reference only; any overt or blatant reading of index cards will result in disqualification.

4. The use of a lectern and/or microphones is optional.

5. The use of visual or media aids is not permitted.

6. Students should consider the two most important items when writing their speech:

   a) What is the entertainment value of their speech?

   b) What is the informational value of their speech?

7. The best speeches are supported by research.

8. Speeches are to last longer than three minutes and not more than five minutes.

9. Dress is to be informal at the class level but formal at the school level.

10. Judging will be based on seven objective criteria by using the form included (Figure 3–2). These criteria are described as follows:

    a) Voice—Attention will be paid to the clarity and volume of the speaker's voice.

    b) Physical appearance—In this category the judges assess the poise, stance and mannerisms or gestures of the speaker.

    c) Organization—The judges will look at the aspects of the development of the speech from introduction to conclusion.

    d) Language—This is a judgment of the quality of English used in the areas of grammar and pronunciation.

e) Manner—Manner is the actual delivery of the speech. Such things as enthusiasm and assurance are judged in this category.

f) Speech value—The ideas, information and impressiveness are judged in speech value.

g) Effectiveness—This criterion concentrates on how well the speech achieved its purpose. Students will be judged on how well the speech kept the interest of, and to what extent it was received by, the audience.

It is best if you use objective judges. That is, you should choose other teachers, administrators, members of the community or public speakers' clubs to be your judges. This will eliminate any bias on your part or on the part of anyone who regularly interacts with the students.

(Figure 3–2)

ORATORY COMPETITION

TOPIC: _____   STUDENT NAME: _____

	EXCELL-ENT	GOOD	FAIR	POOR	CONSTRUCTIVE COMMENTS
VOICE volume and clarity	10	8	6	4	
PHYSICAL poise and gestures	10	8	6	4	
ORGANIZATION how the speech developed from introduction to conclusion	10	8	6	4	
LANGUAGE grammar and pronunciation quality	10	8	6	4	
MANNER degree of enthusiasm and assurance in the delivery	10	8	6	4	
SPEECH VALUE how impressive the speech is in terms of ideas and information	10	8	6	4	
EFFECTIVENESS extent to which speech achieved its purpose, kept interest and was received by the audience	10	8	6	4	
TOTAL					

39. THE BEST BIBLIOGRAPHY FORM IN THE BUSINESS

Problem: You are teaching an English or Language Arts class and you would like the class to do some research. In the process you want the students to learn and use the proper bibliography form. How do you help the students organize and coordinate the necessary data into the most universally recognized bibliography style?

Solution: Use the Bibliography Sheet (Figure 3–3). This sheet is comprehensive in that it shows how to develop the proper bibliography style for the three major sources of written information.

The first form is how a bibliography of a book should be presented. This book form is the most universal and common style.

The second bibliography style is that used for encyclopedias. There are obvious differences from the book form. Again, this style is the most universal.

The third form used here is for magazines. Each source of information is different in its format and therefore needs its own individual style of bibliography form.

The student is to fill in the blank spaces on the form with the information from the resource and then translate that information into a replica of the example given below each form. Normally, students would place a completed bibliography at the end of their essay, report or other written work.

(Figure 3–3)

BIBLIOGRAPHY SHEET

BOOK FORM

Author _____ , _____
              Last Name   First Name and/or Initials

Title (underlined) _____

Place of Publication: _____

Publisher: _____

Date Published: _____

Pages Used: _____

e.g., Petreshene, Susan S. Mind Joggers. West Nyack, New York: The Center for Applied Research in Education, 1986. pp. 17-28.

****

ENCYCLOPEDIA FORM

Author (if given) _____ , _____
                        Last Name   First Name and/or Initials

Title of Article _____
                          In Quotation Marks

Name of Encyclopedia (underlined) _____

Edition (year): _____ Volume: _____ Pages Used: _____

e.g., Smith, Jack L. "Figs." S and S Encyclopedia, 1994, Vol. 7, pp. 82-84.

****

MAGAZINE FORM

Author _____ , _____
              Last Name   First Name and/or Initials

Title of Article _____
                          In Quotation Marks

Name of Magazine _____
                                      Underlined

Volume Number: _____ Pages Used: _____ Date Issued: _____

e.g., Henry, John T. "How to Teach Music." Music Expert 98 (September 1995): 42-47.

40. THE DESK ISLAND SYSTEM

Problem: You find that when student desks are in rows, there is a very inefficient use of space. The problem becomes even more noticeable when you walk from desk to desk helping students. How do you increase teacher access to students while minimizing student misbehavior?

Solution: Place desks in islands of two, three or four. This idea makes walking around the room much easier as there is more efficient use of space.

You will find that as you "float" from island to island and help one person at an island, you are actually helping four persons in that group. This also cuts down on your need to re-explain concepts to each individual student.

When the desks are placed in islands, the general decorum of the classroom is improved as the students are focused upon their "island" and not so much influenced by the behavior of the larger class group.

With desk islands, it is more difficult for a merrymaker or misbehavior specialist to get an audience. Therefore, you have greater control.

Students grouped in this way can help each other. The nature of the groups can be managed by you so that the more able students are equally dispersed.

This will serve to more fully develop the skills of the weaker students as well as reinforce those who are more advanced.

41. PHONE THE TEACHER

Problem: Your math students are coming to you saying "I could not do my homework because there was no one at home who could help me."

Solution: Allow the students to phone you for help in the evening. This will eliminate the above situation because you can easily give directions over the phone on how to solve math (or other) problems. The amount of time taken out of your 'evening' is minimal and will be more than worthwhile when you get to the math class the next day.

It helps the student by alleviating the frustration of working on an assignment he or she does not understand.

This is also an important PR tool. Many parents are more than pleased when their child can phone the teacher after hours for help. They see the alleviation of frustration happening before their eyes. This is a service not offered by many in teaching for various and valid reasons, but if you can do it the rewards certainly are real.

One final note: You will need to set parameters on this. Tell the students the days you are available and what hours are convenient for you.

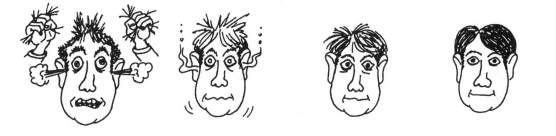

A lot of parent frustration will be alleviated if their child is allowed to phone the teacher.

42. THE GREAT RACE AROUND THE ROOM

Problem: Students at the elementary level need a goal-focusing tool. The children need a program that will provide viable goals. These goals must be tangible and attainable even for the least skilled member of the group.

What can you use as a positive behavior-enhancing device that will become the focal point of the class as well as maintain the students' interest throughout the school year?

Solution: Use "The Great Race Around the Room." Place a white band of paper about a yard/meter wide around the whole classroom. This band of paper must be separated into eight to twelve sections with a vertical line at the end of each section. These vertical lines are called Reward Stations. Give each student a paper car (Figure 3–4) with his or her name on it. Students will place their cars on the starting line on the first day of school. Students are then told they are to move their car along the race track to the reward stations where you will provide a prize. Tell the students there are a number of ways they can help move their car.

It is at this point you introduce your criteria or "fuel" for moving the cars along the white paper race track. That "fuel" is the good or positive ways of behaving or performing in the school and in the classroom. You then list those exact behaviors and performance expectations you want targeted.

Special care must be given to those students of low skills or abilities to make sure their car does not lag behind the others.

The size of the race track and the bright color of the cars will keep The Great Race Around the Room in the students' consciousness throughout the day. You will see students seeking out positive behaviors in order to move their car.

Students are highly competitive, and it is this nature you tap into here. They will see this race track as a source of excitement if your rewards are tangible and of value.

(Figure 3–4)

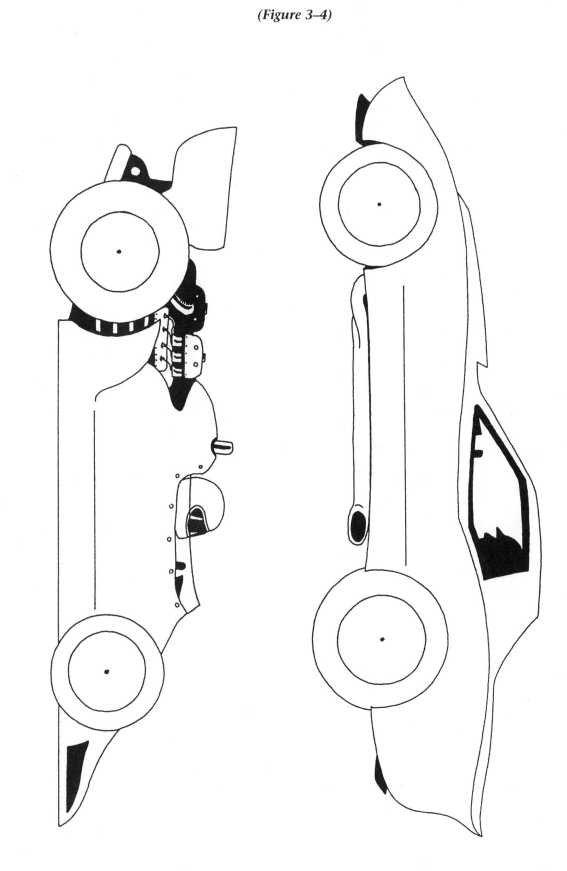

43. THE SCORE CHART

Problem: Students do not have a conscious awareness of how they are doing from week to week or from assignment to assignment. How do you keep students mindful of their performance in a subject?

Solution: When you want the students to know at a glance how well they are performing in spelling or math, have them fill in the Score Chart (Figure 3–5). This chart is based on a test of twenty questions. Students are told that each correct answer is worth five percent.

If a student answered seventeen questions correctly in the first assignment or test, then he or she would put an X or a circle on 85% for assignment or test number one. If the student answered twelve questions correctly on the second test or assignment, then the student would circle or put an X on 60% for assignment number two and so on for all the assignments.

The student should draw a line from one assignment or test score to another in order. This would, in effect, provide the student and the teacher with an easy-to-read graph of the student's performance. This chart/graph has three features beyond being a progress indicator. These are:

a) If an assignment was missed, it would be obvious to the student. He or she would, therefore, know to make arrangements to get caught up.

b) Students will gain an understanding of number-percent relationships.

c) The chart itself can be adapted for use with most subjects in order to graph the student's performance in those areas.

The Score Chart allows parents to gain a quick understanding of how well their child is performing at any given point in time.

It is possible to derive a term grade from the average of all the marks on a student's Score Chart if you feel it is appropriate to do so.

(Figure 3–5)

ASSIGNMENT NUMBER

SCORE CHART

	1	2	3	4	5	6	7	8	9	10	11	12	13	14	15	16	17	18
20	100	100	100	100	100	100	100	100	100	100	100	100	100	100	100	100	100	100
19	95	95	95	95	95	95	95	95	95	95	95	95	95	95	95	95	95	95
18	90	90	90	90	90	90	90	90	90	90	90	90	90	90	90	90	90	90
17	85	85	85	85	85	85	85	85	85	85	85	85	85	85	85	85	85	85
16	80	80	80	80	80	80	80	80	80	80	80	80	80	80	80	80	80	80
15	75	75	75	75	75	75	75	75	75	75	75	75	75	75	75	75	75	75
14	70	70	70	70	70	70	70	70	70	70	70	70	70	70	70	70	70	70
13	65	65	65	65	65	65	65	65	65	65	65	65	65	65	65	65	65	65
12	60	60	60	60	60	60	60	60	60	60	60	60	60	60	60	60	60	60
11	55	55	55	55	55	55	55	55	55	55	55	55	55	55	55	55	55	55
10	50	50	50	50	50	50	50	50	50	50	50	50	50	50	50	50	50	50
9	45	45	45	45	45	45	45	45	45	45	45	45	45	45	45	45	45	45
8	40	40	40	40	40	40	40	40	40	40	40	40	40	40	40	40	40	40
7	35	35	35	35	35	35	35	35	35	35	35	35	35	35	35	35	35	35
6	30	30	30	30	30	30	30	30	30	30	30	30	30	30	30	30	30	30
5	25	25	25	25	25	25	25	25	25	25	25	25	25	25	25	25	25	25
4	20	20	20	20	20	20	20	20	20	20	20	20	20	20	20	20	20	20
3	15	15	15	15	15	15	15	15	15	15	15	15	15	15	15	15	15	15
2	10	10	10	10	10	10	10	10	10	10	10	10	10	10	10	10	10	10
1	5	5	5	5	5	5	5	5	5	5	5	5	5	5	5	5	5	5
0	0	0	0	0	0	0	0	0	0	0	0	0	0	0	0	0	0	0

NUMBER CORRECT (left axis)

% SCORES FOR NUMBER CORRECT

The completed SCORE CHART will look like this.

44. FRAME OF REFERENCE CHART

Problem: How can the teacher keep the parents from assuming that the tests you give are too difficult for everyone? How can you give a quick visual frame of reference to the parents that tells them where their child's score is in relation to the average grade as well as to the high and low marks in the class?

Solution: After tests have been graded, write all the marks in order on the Frame of Reference Chart (Figure 3–6). Then indicate the average test mark with a line. Circle the student's mark. Draw a line from the student's test score to his or her name.

Individual sheets are then sent to the parents. This is an excellent tool to use for parent-teacher conferences. It will show all concerned the range of marks attained on the test as well as an individual's standing.

(Figure 3–6)

FRAME OF REFERENCE CHART

_____   _____
          TEST NAME   DATE OF TEST

- -

**HIGH
SCORE**   _____

                _____

                _____

                _____

                _____

                _____

                _____

                _____   Student's Name: _____

                _____   Average Grade: _____

                _____

                _____

                _____

                _____

                _____

                _____

                _____

                _____

                _____

                _____

**LOW
SCORE**   _____

                _____

45. TEST-TYPE QUESTIONS

Problem: When students are to take a test in a subject where the answers on the test must be exact and absolute, how do you familiarize students with the correct data to concentrate on when preparing for that test?

Solution: Create a "test type" question sheet for students to practice.

These test-type questions are not designed to give away what is on the test but rather to give a "ballpark" idea of what they are expected to know.

The sheet of test-type questions should include the page numbers from which the data is taken. This will allow the student at home to refer to examples and variations of other questions on those pages.

The test-type questions will inform you of weak areas in your students before testing occurs. It will allow you to phone a parent to inform him or her of those areas to watch for.

46. NOTICE-OF-MATERIALS-RECEIVED SHEET

Problem: Frequently students lose materials, especially those study handouts that are being used by you from which a test or quiz will be developed. Some students will tell their parents that you never gave the materials to them in the first place. (Sound familiar?) This statement seems to increase in frequency the night before your test.

With today's larger classrooms and multi-resource based learning, it is almost impossible to really confirm at a moment's notice whether Judy or Jack did obtain your handouts. This problem is especially acute when you receive an angry parent's phone call asking why his or her child did not get the necessary data from you. How do you protect yourself from the frustrated misinformed parent?

Solution: Have the students sign the Notice-of-Materials-Received Sheet. (Figure 3–7). This sheet is signed by all students immediately after receiving a package of materials from you.

The Notice Sheet will help you not only when it becomes necessary to prove to a parent that you did indeed give his or her child the information from which to develop a report or to study from, but it will also aid you in keeping a record of those who did not get the package of materials. This allows you to make sure those missing from the list are given the data in time to do the work you require.

You should number the material packages you give out. It adds a bit more credibility to your position if you can show parents that not only did the student sign for the materials he needed to study for your test, he received package number 26.

Few parents will disagree with the signed "Notice-of-Materials-Received Sheet." This sheet gives the student 100% ownership of the problem if the information gets lost.

(Figure 3–7)

NOTICE-OF-MATERIALS-RECEIVED SHEET

Date: _____   Subject: _____   Teacher: _____

I have received the following instructional materials _____

_____

*I understand that instruction, report, essays, tests and questions may be developed from these materials.

*Sign your name beside the number assigned to your materials package.

- -

1. _____

2. _____

3. _____

4. _____

5. _____

6. _____

7. _____

8. _____

9. _____

10. _____

11. _____

12. _____

13. _____

14. _____

15. _____

16. _____

17. _____

18. _____

19. _____

20. _____

21. _____

22. _____

23. _____

24. _____

25. _____

26. _____

27. _____

28. _____

29. _____

30. _____

31. _____

32. _____

33. _____

34. _____

Best Suited for
Grade 4 to High School

47. STAGGER DUE DATES FOR ASSIGNMENTS

Problem: Many students do not hand in assignments on time. In today's culture there are many reasons for this, some valid and some not. How do you help students finish their work within a certain time frame? How do you get all the work in for grading by a specific day and yet be flexible in terms of understanding the students' various circumstances?

Solution: When you assign an essay, report, or other assignment to a class do not have one specific day when the work is required to be handed in to you. Tell the students that the work is due in on Monday, Tuesday, or Wednesday—not just on Monday as you would normally have done.

There are several advantages to staggering the due date of the assignments:

a) You more than likely would not get to look at all of the assignments that first day anyway. You can spread your work out over time.

b) This should alleviate the problem of late hand-ins. The type of student who would usually be late handing in his or her assignment now has a more compatible (for them) time frame within which to operate.

c) Staggering the due day will allow you to upgrade (if you so desire) or reward those better students who would normally give you the assignment on time or even before the due date of the report or essay. That reward system would operate when you tell the students that you are going to automatically upgrade by X% those assignments that came in on or before the first due day of the assignment. All work that came in on the other due days would simply get the regular mark and no upgrading would take place. Another form of upgrading would be to offer a certain descending percent of upgrading for each day the work is due. For example, if the work is due on Monday a bonus of 5% is given for all work handed in on or before that day. A bonus of 4% is given for the work handed in on Tuesday, 3% for Wednesday and so on. On the last day no upgrade bonus is given. With this system I would state that because of the generous nature of the upgrading plan, those students who are late would get an automatic grade of "D" after the final due date. These upgrading systems tend to justifiably reward the better students who usually have their work in early or on time.

48. ALPHABET PORRIDGE

Problem: You want to stimulate language development in your subject area. Is there a tool that is interesting and therefore self-propelling that will help develop vocabulary? It is important that this tool not require a great deal of preparation time.

Solution: Divide your class into groups of 3 or 4. Give them a copy of the Alphabet Porridge Sheet (Figure 3–8). Name a category such as animals, plants, rivers or health. Give them a time limit and let them go.

The sheet is scored on the basis of how many words in the subject area, starting with each letter of the alphabet, the group can think of. They get 5 points for the first word, 3 for the second, 2 for the third and 1 for the fourth. A maximum of 11 points for each letter is available.

Have them add up their score at the end of the time limit.

The teacher can allow the use of resource books.

I have found this to be a great activity to use when the students are nearing the end of a unit of work on "Cities of the World," for example. The Alphabet Porridge game heightens interest and awareness because it requires concentration to complete while providing a degree of competition among groups of students.

You will notice that the students will get really quiet during the competition because they don't want members of the other groups stealing their ideas.

Alphabet Porridge is one of the best ways to enhance vocabulary development in a specific subject area as well as to have a great deal of genuine fun with the learning process.

(Figure 3–8)

ALPHABET PORRIDGE SHEET

	5	3	2	1	Total
A					
B					
C					
D					
E					
F					
G					
H					
I					
J					
K					
L					
M					
N					
O					
P					
Q					
R					
S					
T					
U					
V					
W					
X					
Y					
Z					
				SCORE	

49. CLASS HOMEWORK BOOK

Problem: Students forget what homework they have been assigned during a school day. This is especially true if students have had a different teacher for each class. How do you make the students aware of what homework has been assigned at the end of each day when there is a strong likelihood you will not have that class in the last period?

Solution: Create a Class Homework Book that is read to the students at the end of each school day. This homework book will allow teachers of different subjects to write down what homework is required for their subject area. Each page of the homework book (Figure 3–9) provides all of the necessary information areas for students.

This works best with a homogenous class that stays together for most of the school day.

It is a good idea to have one of the more reliable students carry the Class Homework Book from one class to another. The last teacher of the day for each class will read the list of assignments in the homework book to the students, thereby reminding them of what work is due and when.

(Figure 3–9)

CLASS HOMEWORK ASSIGNMENTS

DATE: _____

	SUBJECT	ASSIGNMENT	DATE DUE
1			
2			
3			
4			
5			
6			
7			
8			

50. GIMME A SHOE FOR A PEN

Problem: There is not a teacher in all of recorded history who has not been confronted with the "I don't have a pen or pencil" problem. Many students (intentional or otherwise) arrive at class without the necessary writing, drawing or geometry equipment.

It is a poor economy to send the student home or even to his or her locker for the materials as this disrupts the class and causes the student to miss a portion of the lesson.

You could loan the pen, pencil or other equipment to the student; however, there is no guarantee you will ever see that material again. This problem is especially acute if there is a rush of events at the end of a class.

Solution: When a student needs materials from your teacher's supply, you lend it to that student. However, as you give it, you ask the student to donate one of his or her shoes in trade for the equipment. You tell the student that you will give the shoe back when the pen, pencil, compass, protractor or whatever is returned to you.

The only slight logistical problem you may have with this idea is finding a good place to store a smelly sneaker or two. I find that a proper sized cardboard box with a lid solves the storage problem quite nicely.

The beauty of this idea is that it will most certainly guarantee you a 100% return of your equipment or materials. There are not many students who would walk to the next class with only one shoe.

51. THE RED LINE

Problem: Many times students have trouble working on written material through a whole period. In the large classes of today, it is difficult for the teacher to be everywhere at once.

How do you get students to keep on task yet, at the same time, give you instant feedback as to how much written work they have accomplished? How can you give a child a frame of reference from which to perform?

Solution: Some ideas are very simple and yet extremely effective. The Red Line falls into this category.

Before you start your work period, go to those students you choose (usually the tardy ones) and make a red line under the last bit of work they have completed. Tell these students that you want to see "performance" beyond the red line. You may find it necessary in some cases to initial the red line.

This red line will give you and the student a reference point from which to judge how much work that student has completed at any point in the period. A one-second glance at the student's paper will tell you the volume of work the student has been able to do.

The red line stares the student right in the face. It tells him or her that he or she better have something to show beyond the line.

After a while students will bring their notebooks up to you and ask you to put the red line on their paper. It shows you care and in return their work shows they care.

52. THE VIDEO SHEET

Problem: You show videos to your students to reinforce learning. You want them to have the maximum focus on the presentation. You desire your students to logically analyze the video or pick out the data that is of use to them. You could create a series of questions on the information in the video but that has its own inherent problems. What is the most efficient way for your students to use the visual presentation?

Solution: Have the students complete a Video Sheet when they watch the video (Figure 3–10).

In the first or "Good" box, the students write those aspects of the video or movie that they consider to be good or of some positive value.

In the second or "Not So Good/Ordinary" box, the students write those things they observed in the presentation that were not good, or just ordinary, from their point of view.

The Video Sheet has several attractive features:

1. It allows the students to be creative in their individual analysis of the video or movie. This in itself can lead to later discussions, brainstorming and so forth.

2. There is virtually no preparation for the teacher as there would be with a series of questions.

3. Not only can answers not be missed but talking during the video will be minimized because no one is asking other students for an answer to a missed question.

4. The number of responses is at the discretion of the teacher.

© 1996 by The Center for Applied Research in Education

(Figure 3–10)

THE VIDEO SHEET

Name: _____   Date: _____

Name of Video: _____

1. In the GOOD box list those aspects of the video or film that you feel are positive or worthwhile.

2. In the NOT SO GOOD / ORDINARY box list those aspects of the video that you feel are negative or just ordinary.

GOOD

NOT SO GOOD / ORDINARY

53. VOCABULARY CHAINS

Problem: You want to reinforce your teaching in an area such as history or science. You would like the students to enjoy learning the vocabulary of your subject area. How can you heighten interest in the words and language of your unit?

Solution: Use the Vocabulary Chains (Figure 3–11). The student uses the words from the subject area to fill in the chains. The unique thing about the chains is that students are to think of a word from their subject area that would start with the last letter from the previous word. For example: In a history chain, if a student wrote WASHINGTON in the first link of the chain, then the next word to follow in the next link would start with the N of WASHINGTON and so on.

You may decide to have students work independently at their desks on the chains or it can be made into a game with groups of three or four students competing against each other to see who would be first to fill in the links.

Some students or groups of students may be able to complete all the links of the chain from memory but most will not; therefore, it is a good idea to provide some sort of resource, such as a textbook or map, for the students' reference. If you do use resource materials, you will find it necessary to restrict the use of indexes in order to make the learning process as profitable as possible for the students.

(Figure 3–11)

VOCABULARY CHAIN

NAME:_____

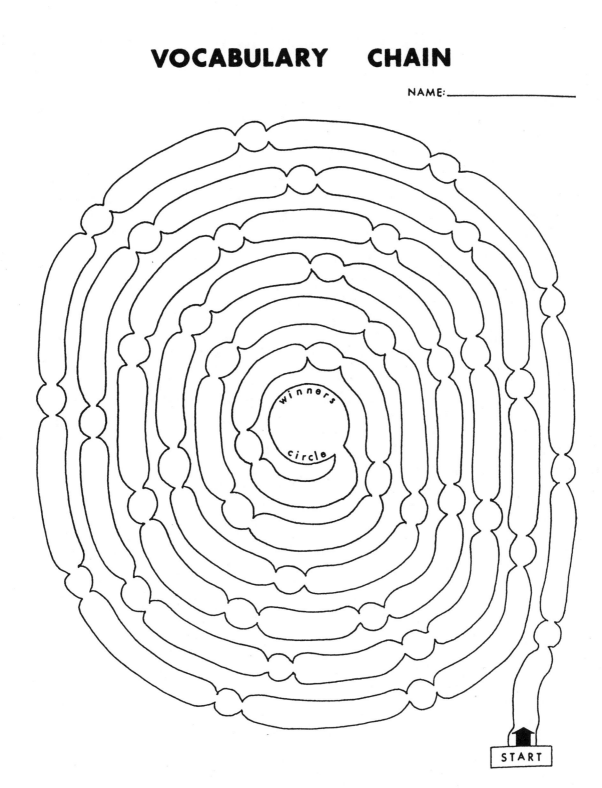

54. CRITICAL ANALYSIS SHEET

Problem: Most teachers have a variety of students in their classrooms. The range of intellectual skills can be quite wide with greatly differing needs developing from that diversity.

The mandate of the teacher is to present the curriculum to everyone. This will sometimes mean working at the pace of the slower persons, thus creating problems at the other end. The intellectually aggressive students will stagnate in boredom and perhaps even become behavior problems because they are ahead of the norm of students.

How do you quickly alleviate boredom in the brighter students when you must still help the others?

Solution: Give the bored student(s) the Critical Analysis Sheet (Figure 3–12). This sheet is unique in that it requires no preparation on your part (other than photocopying). It requires no forewarning of boredom occurring. It is highly directive and leads to later discussion.

What you need to do is provide a topic for the students to work on. The topic should be of a more open or controversial nature, such as war or the ozone level. The brighter students will recognize the enrichment value of the critical analysis topic and will, by nature, work on it very enthusiastically.

It is best to give the same topic to two or more students at the same time. Students are to research independently, in encyclopedias or library materials, for the first time frame. They are to gather as many pro and con perspectives as possible.

Once students have obtained a sufficient amount of data, they should be grouped together to present their views on the topic to each other in the second time frame. In this way, the Critical Analysis Sheet creates directed group discussion on a topic of the teacher's choice. The students now are no longer bored and you, the teacher, are free to help others who have needs.

(Figure 3–12)

CRITICAL ANALYSIS SHEET

Issue _____

PRO	CON

Value Judgment/Conclusion

Was the data of sufficient quality and quantity in order to give validity to your judgment?

55. THE RESEARCH PAPER

Problem: Students need to have direction when preparing to do research in a subject area. The more explicit or clear the directions for the work, the more likely the teacher is to get quality feedback from his or her students.

How do you inform students of exactly what you want in order to ensure honest, consistent and reliable responses from the students?

Solution: Give the students the research paper form (Figure 3–13) This form tells the students exactly what you want and the fact that they will be graded according to your set requirements. The research paper form is self explanatory and has been designed to be as universal as possible.

Each research paper handed to you is to have a formal title page and must be two pages in length in this case. A bibliography is needed as well as a diagram of the topic, and of course the paper must be a well-groomed production.

Note-taking sheets are included here for a specific reason. These sheets are a reasonably true indicator that the student actually did the work of researching the topic. These notes, rough as they may be, will indicate to you that the student did the work.

Some people will say that a rough copy of the paper will also indicate whether or not the work was performed by that student. This is not always the case because some students are quite capable of creating the good copy directly from the research notes, thus eliminating the necessity of having a rough copy.

(Figure 3–13)

RESEARCH PAPER

Choose one of the topics below and prepare a research paper. Each paper should include and will be graded on:

1. A Formal Title Page

2. Note-taking Sheet(s)

3. Research Paper
   - 2 pages typed, 3-4 pages neat handwriting
   - double spaced
   - include an Introduction (introduces or outlines what you are going to write about. Start with an interesting fact or a related story.)

4. Bibliography
   - you need 4 sources, rough copy (sheet given), and a good copy (follow example given)

5. Drawing or Diagram
   - ach paper must have at least one drawing or diagram
   - no photocopies

6. Neatness
   - double spaced, neatly handwritten, typed or word processed on clean white paper

TOPICS:

1. _____

2. _____

3. _____

4. _____

TOPIC OF YOUR CHOICE APPROVED BY TEACHER

56. HYPOTHESIS BOXES

Problem: You want to teach the concept of hypothesis formation because understanding this is central to any scientific experiment or study.

You could say a hypothesis is a tentative assertion to be worked through, or you could state that it is a proposition assumed as a basis for reasoning, but these definitions are often vague for my grade eights.

What you want to do is cause students to use stimulus input to infer, deduce, analyze and reason, in order to produce that tentative assertion or proposed assumption about the things or events under study. This is the hypothesis.

How do I teach a difficult concept like hypothesis formation to students who need the idea translated to their level of understanding?

How can I make the students use senses other than sight to gather evidence for preparing a hypothesis?

Solution: Prepare hypothesis boxes. Get ten or fifteen boxes about the size of a chalk box or 4" × 4" × 4". These boxes must be made of fairly heavy cardboard in order to be durable. Gather different common objects (e.g., erasers) from home or school and place one item in each box. (One of the boxes should contain a heavily scented perfume bottle.) After making sure each item in the boxes is loose and free to move around inside, seal each box with masking tape. Place a large number on each box. On a separate sheet of paper, record what objects you placed in what number box.

Have the students take one box at a time and record the number of each box they work with. Students are then asked to write down all the evidence that their senses can ascertain that would indicate what type of object is inside each box. Figure 3–14 is provided for this purpose.

After all students have worked through all the ten or fifteen boxes, you put the list of items that are in the boxes in random order on the board. Students are then to make an educated guess from their evidence to formulate a tentative assertion or hypothesis as to what is in each box.

With this idea, hypothesis formation becomes real or concrete for students. Students should be told that logical deductive reasoning is the key to any experiment and therefore to any hypothesis development.

© 1996 by The Center for Applied Research in Education

(Figure 3–14)

HYPOTHESIS BOX RECORD SHEET

Date: _____   Class: _____   Name:_____

Number	Evidence From Senses	Educated Guess
1		
2		
3		
4		
5		
6		
7		
8		
9		
10		
11		
12		
13		
14		
15		

57. THE PRIMARY PAIL ORGANIZER

Problem: Your primary students are in need of some kind of organizer when they first come into the classroom.

You find that while they have hangers for their coats, everything else gets scattered, lost or stolen. Lockers would be useful, but the children are too young to maintain a locker with a combination or a key.

How can you help young, primary students "keep it all together"?

Solution: Use plastic ice cream pails with the student's name on them. The pails should be placed on a shelf directly above the student's coat hanger. Any miscellaneous items that belong to the child, such as crayons, pencils and erasers could be kept in the ice cream pail.

The idea here is to keep the pails on a shelf so that the student will have to bring the pail down to put his or her materials into it. If the pails were lower, there is a likelihood that Johnny's pencils would end up in Susie's pail or vice versa. If the pails are just within reach, there is less temptation to put things in another person's pail.

Whether or not you use the lids on the pail is purely up to you. Some classes are mature enough to easily remove the lid, while others are not.

The use of the student's personal pail can have added advantages for you. If you want to send a note or letter home to the parents, the pail can be used as a mailbox. You simply place the letters in the pails at any time during the day. This is especially important for classes that are team taught or when a note giver cannot be there at the end of a school day when messages would normally be given out.

58. THE CLASSROOM ROUTINE

Problem: In many elementary schools, students need to have a regular pattern of behaviors in order to know when and how to function.

How do you structure your school day to make it work for the maximum in behavior control?

Solution: Consciously make the day's periods into a series of routines with expected behaviors in those routines.

There are key times in the school day when the routine is most necessary for maximum learning and behavior control. These key times are at the start of classes in the morning, immediately after recesses and after the noon hour break.

If you have the same subjects taught at these times each day, the students soon get used to the routine. It is important that a series of expected behaviors are adhered to during these routine classes. For example, when students enter your class on any morning, it is expected that they immediately get out their math notebooks and work on the questions you have put on the board. This expected response will be automatic with every child if you consciously set up the routine system. This routine becomes the normal way to act for everybody, and therefore class behavior problems will be at a minimum. No student will be confused or lacking knowledge as to what he or she should do. This is the beauty of this concept. Students do not like to feel unsure of what they are to do next. With the routine, everyone has a place and is comfortable with what they are expected to do.

It may take a while for the younger students to adapt to the routine but, with consistent coaching each day, even the most needy student will come to profit from this idea.

59. THE ORGANIZER SCRAPBOOK

Problem: Your primary or elementary grade students have difficulty keeping their work together. Many times you find important assignments on the floor or scattered in every direction.

How can you keep the students' work organized and presentable for you to evaluate and for the parents to see?

Solution: Have your students glue their work into a large scrapbook. When an important assignment is completed, students will automatically reach for their scrapbook and attach the work in there as a matter of routine.

It is up to you whether you want to keep the pile of scrapbooks under your watchful eye. You may prefer to let the students keep them in their desks or storage areas. In any event, the scrapbook should not leave the classroom for the duration of the school year. The scrapbook, therefore, is the storage place for completed assignments and not a workbook to be taken home.

The scrapbook is ideal when it comes time for parent-teacher conferences. The student's work is organized and glued in place for all to see.

It may be advisable, depending on your circumstances, to section off the scrapbook for specific subject areas.

Most students will fill up more than two scrapbooks per year, so it is advisable to maintain a good storage area for finished scrapbooks.

60. THE BACK-TO-BACK ESSAY REVIEW IDEA

Problem: Students often feel they have no ownership of what is happening to them in the classroom.

How can you cause the students to have some real involvement in the preparation and development of a review program?

Solution: Use the Back-to-Back Essay Review for the students. With this idea, the students work in pairs to develop up to two essay questions each, for a total of four, for an upcoming review. The students hand in their set of four questions to the teacher. The quality of the questions is then evaluated to see if they are okay for the review.

When it comes time for the review to be given to the class, all the students are given a regular set of questions prepared by the teacher. Along with the regular set, the teacher gives back to each pair of students the four questions they developed together. This means that if normally a review was to be ten questions, then the teacher would prepare six and the review would be completed by adding the four student questions. They now know at least four questions that are going to be on the review.

When the pair of students answers the questions, they do not sit facing each other but rather they sit back to back. One student is called Student A and the other is called Student B. Student A is given half the review or five questions, and Student B is given the other half of the review or the other five questions. When both students have done as much as they can on their set of five questions, they put their initials on the work they have done, then they pass their set of answers and questions to their partners. When Students A and B have exchanged questions and answers, they then seek to improve their partner's answers.

When improvements have been made, the improvements are also initialed by the student who does the improving. The initialing is necessary to insure that one of the two students doesn't do all the work.

This type of review allows the student a degree of ownership, and as such, it is a great reinforcer of the material you are teaching. It causes students to think and cooperate.

61. THE GREAT LETTER TOOL

Problem: You have a fresh group of students in grade one. You must initiate them into the wonders and skills of reading and writing.

What is an excellent proven method of teaching the importance of written communication, as well as developing the skills necessary in this area?

Solution: Use the old-fashioned written letter form.

About a week before school begins send a letter to each of the students registered in your class welcoming them. Tell the student how much you are looking forward to having him or her in your classroom.

For the first week or two write several letters to the parents describing the ongoing function of your classroom. Make it clear to the parents that you are grateful for the opportunity to guide their child down the path of knowledge and education. In this way, the child will become accustomed to the importance of letters as a means of communication, and the parents will see that you are genuinely concerned about their child's welfare.

Each and every day from the start of school you should write a letter on the blackboard or on an experience chart. The first printing lessons can begin from here. Students can get "hands on" experience by copying the letter either on the blackboard or on copy paper.

Reading skills will begin to soar if you use this format consistently. The letter always has the same style of greeting, body, closing and signature. Students see this form every day and, with new content to the body of the letter, all students will have an enhanced desire to *read* the contents.

In the first weeks of school, you will have to read the letter while hand scanning the words. It will not be long before the "sharpies" will be able to read some words. In most grade one classes, there are one or two early readers who will amaze you with their ability.

You will find that if you keep the format of your letters simple and similar, it will not take long before the whole class is reading the whole letter.

After a few weeks of reading, it becomes time to expand the use of the letter in order to teach those skill areas that are necessary for the development of excellent readers and writers.

Some ideas in the teaching of reading, writing and communications skills are:

1. Word recognition

   a)   Ask a child to find a word he or she can read on the letter that is on the blackboard. Have the child read the word out loud, then erase the word from the board. Our goal would then be to eventually erase the complete letter; thus having read all the words.

   b)   Ask the children to find specific words and circle them.

   c)   Choose two children of approximately equal ability and see who can find the required word first (children love competition).

2. Phonetic Study

    a)   Ask children to find words that begin with the same letter.

    b)   Have students look for words with the same vowel.

3. Word Analysis

    a)   Ask students to circle words with certain endings.

    b)   Have students try to recognize shortest and longest words.

4. Punctuation and capitalization skills become easy to teach as a natural function of the letter form.

5. The correct structure of friendly or business letters is learned at an early age.

6. Special events in the school, birthdays or important achievements can be announced in the daily letter on the board.

7. Children will feel comfortable using the letter form as a model when they begin writing.

8. Letter writing can be used to initiate creative writing, e.g., letter to Santa, storybook characters or famous people.

9. It is interesting to have the students write a letter from another person's point of view, i.e., from the perspective of a firefighter during fire safety week or from the angle of a dentist during dental week.

10. Have a Gobbledegook Day with the letter form. On this day you change the order and mix up the letter parts or omit the punctuation and capitalization on the letter as it appears on the blackboard. With this gobbledegooked letter, the children would then assist you in correcting the form.

11. In the letter form you can introduce an endless variety of new and challenging words for the students to decode. This vocabulary expansion, as you know, is a key to understanding concepts.

12. As a final activity for the school year, it is a great idea to have your class write a welcoming letter for next year's grade one's. This final activity completes your letter use plan for the year, and it brings the grade one's full circle into grade two.

★ 4 ★

NEAT AND FUN THINGS TO DO IN SCHOOL

Neat and Fun Things to Do in School will add some genuine delight to your teaching days. The creative ideas revealed in this section reduce teacher stress by increasing positive interactions among the students, teachers and the community.

Many of the concepts require little if any preparation, other than photocopying the forms we provide.

62. THE COMMUNITY SERVICE P.R. AND GOLD CARD PROGRAM

Problem: You want to teach responsibility to the teenagers in your school. You would like that responsibility to be community based or directed.

How can you reach out from the microcosm of the school to the larger community in order to teach a sense of responsibility to your students?

Solution: Tie community service to being a member of your school's team. Usually sports and nonsports (debating) teams are high interest and high status around a high school. In order to develop a sense of responsibility in those players, make it a prerequisite that each team member performs some sort of visible community service as part of being a member of the team. For example, the football team players (because football is played in the fall of the year) could work at pre-winter yard cleanup for senior citizens.

The volleyball team could volunteer to canvass for the Kidney Foundation and the basketball team could repaint a community day-care facility.

Some community service would have to be keyed to the time of year. For example, the Heart Fund usually collects money around the beginning of February, so the team that is in action at that time could canvass for them. Other organizations, such as groups that deliver meals or groceries to "shut-ins," need help all year round.

It is an excellent idea to have the young people in your school focus on helping the seniors in your community. As the students clean yards or paint fences for the elderly people in your community, have the captain of the team that is doing the service give the senior citizen a gold card pass. This gold card pass would allow senior citizens to attend for free any of the team's games that occur at your school.

One school I know of gave out the gold cards, and as part of the community service, they have to drive those seniors to and from their games.

The P.R. value of this idea is immeasurable. The community group you are helping will spread the word far and wide.

The students gain from the sense of accomplishment and goodwill they have created. The interaction between seniors, the underprivileged, the infirm, and so forth and the students is an added benefit in its own right.

Few other teacher techniques will have such a wide-ranging joyous ripple effect in your community.

119

63. THE GREAT IMPROMPTU SPEECH IDEA

Problem: There are times during the course of any school year when you may not be fully prepared for class. It may be a situation where you are asked to cover a class for another teacher or due to extenuating circumstances, you are confronted with extra time in your own class and have nothing prepared. What do you do with the twenty-eight plus students you have in front of you? How can you use this time wisely?

Solution: Here is one of the most ingenious techniques of them all. Have the students stand up and give impromptu one-minute speeches. Take a piece of plain white paper and tear it up into as many pieces as you can. Write different topics from the subject you are teaching or write several interesting topics (rock music, for example) on the pieces of paper.

The students then choose a topic by the tried-and-true drawing-from-a-hat method. The students should draw their topic at the start of the class so that by the time it gets around to being their turn to speak, they will have given some thought to the topic and, perhaps, even made notes.

It has been my experience that it is not good economy to have the speeches last more than one minute. Most students tend to run out of information around the sixty-second mark. There are exceptions, of course. Some students have the ability to speak for hours on a topic such as toothpicks. The timeframe of one minute is also just about right in terms of allowing enough time in a school period for all students to be able to speak.

This idea will expand everyone's knowledge base on the topics presented. It will help develop those ad lib public speaking skills the students are sure to need in the years to come. It does all this while fulfilling your need to have a lesson for a class.

64. HOW TO PLAY THE STOCK MARKET IN THE CLASSROOM

Problem: You teach in a high socioeconomic area. The students are from affluent families or are from an upwardly mobile class in our culture. What enrichment program will be of high interest to them and will be a part of their real world?

Solution: Introduce the students to the stock market. Most students of the upwardly mobile or affluent classes will have heard their parents at least discuss some of the details of the stock market and, in many cases, the students themselves will have dabbled in stocks and bonds under the direction of their parents.

With the following ideas, you can have the students "obtain" (on paper, that is) stocks the very first day you introduce them to the concepts.

You must prepare some introduction for the first class. I suggest the following topics be covered. They are readily available in any good encyclopedia.

1. What the stocks actually are—part of a company.

2. Why are stocks or shares sold? What is a dividend?

3. What is a stock exchange and how does it function?

Once these basic concepts have been covered, you must teach the students how to read the stock market quotations in the newspaper. For this you will need one copy for each student as the writing is small and therefore a good deal of concentration is needed.

The stock market quotations are usually listed in this order: the name of the company, the volume of shares sold, the high price of the day, the low price of the day, the last or closing price of the day and the net change from the previous day. This must be detailed to the students as each is looking at the actual listings.

After the students understand the layout of the quotations, you tell the students you are going to give them one hundred thousand shares in one or more companies. The students are to choose the company(ies) from the listings and write the name of that company on the stock market form provided (Figure 4–1).

Tell the students they were very sharp when they purchased their shares because they bought them at the low price of that particular day.

In this way you have caused the student to have ownership immediately. These stock purchases by the student should be checked at least once a week. You will find the students will be ravenous for information about "their" companies. You can use the student gains and losses to show the risk nature of the stock market.

Once the students have their share purchases in place, you can then expand their knowledge base by covering some of the following topics:

© 1996 by The Center for Applied Research in Education

1. What is the Dow Jones Industrial Average?
2. What are blue chip stocks?
3. What are bear and bull markets?
4. Why did the stock exchange crash in 1929?

I have found that when this program is used for enrichment with a group of twenty or more students, it is wise to stay with stocks or shares, and not get into bonds, debentures or mutual funds unless specifically requested to do so.

This idea introduces students to the basic design of the ongoing functions of the stock market. The fact that you have given ownership of a significant amount of stocks in a company of their choice will cause the students to develop further insights into the money world. They will often stop you at non-class times to tell you of their gains and losses. You will have no other enrichment program that pays such good dividends.

(Figure 4–1)

STOCK CERTIFICATE

100,000 SHARES

of

_____.

"COMPANY"

COST PER SHARE AT LOWEST PRICE

OF PURCHASE DAY—_____.

PURCHASER _____.

PURCHASE DATE _____.

65. THE LIBRARY AUCTION

Problem: How do you provide incentives to stimulate reading in your library or resource center? How do you help students see the resources you have in the library as objects of value—that reading is important?

Solution: Here is an ingenious idea that will require some logistical legwork on your part. This is the library or resource center auction.

Offer the students Book Bucks (Figure 4–2) for each book they read. At the end of the year (or term), the librarian has an Auction of the goodies he or she has collected throughout the year. The students use the Book Bucks to purchase those objects of value at the auction.

You must establish a set of criteria for payment of the Book Bucks. For example, any book over two hundred pages would be worth one hundred Book Bucks; any book between one hundred and two hundred pages would be worth fifty Book Bucks, and so forth.

You may desire to have your criteria for paying out the Book Bucks based on page value. If a student reads a five-hundred-seventy-seven-page novel, that student would receive five hundred seventy-seven Book Bucks for the end-of-the-term auction. If the student reads a twenty-one-page booklet, then that student would receive twenty-one Book Bucks. The criteria for paying out Book Bucks is at the discretion of the teacher or librarian.

The Book Bucks themselves are designed in such a way as to not be transferable from one student to another or from one year to another. If they become transferable, then they would become almost like legal tender around the school, thus creating a series of problems that you do not need.

The logistical legwork comes in when you must provide the objects to be auctioned off. The type of goodies must be relative to the group of students you are targeting. The prizes to be auctioned off to a group of grade four students would be vastly different from the objects you would offer to a senior high school group.

Objects such as electronic game materials or tickets to the circus may appeal to the lower levels while being a disc jockey at the local radio station or a football signed by the nearest pro team might appeal to the upper level students. The more creative you are in this legwork, the more successful your auction will become.

You must be able to attain these prizes or goods to be auctioned at a minimal or zero cost to you, the teacher. This is done by drawing upon the resources of the community. You must prepare a request letter that explains you are providing an incentive plan for your students and you need help by way of a donation from their organization, store or business.

You will find that even though these people are deluged with requests, they do like to help out educational programs. Your letter of request for prizes should bring in a fifty to sixty percent positive response from your local community.

The Library Auction will become the focal point of the year for the staff of the library as well as the students. You can also use this auction as a high-profile PR event by calling in the local media to tape or photograph the auction. This will do wonders in terms of getting prizes for next year as well as give some deserved publicity to those who donated objects for the auction in the current year.

(*Figure 4–2*)

66. A "MEET THE TEACHER NIGHT" LEARNING EXPERIENCE

Problem: On Meet the Teacher Night, the staff of the school is introduced to the parents in the school gymnasium, and from there, teachers usually go to their respective classrooms followed by a group of up to forty parents each. In this situation, it is expected that the teacher will discuss programs, describe the curriculum and explain school and classroom policies.

How can the teacher utilize the adult captive audience of Meet the Teacher Night as a learning experience for students?

Solution: Once the teacher has completed his or her presentation on policies and procedures, enough time should be made available by the teacher for a group of students to make a presentation about some aspect of the programs he or she is teaching them.

The students will probably, at no other time during the school year, be able to hone public speaking and presentation skills before such a large group of adults. To speak in front of classroom peers is one thing, but to speak to the parents of those peers is a different matter altogether.

It is important that the students not be the main speaker to describe the curriculum and tell about policies. They are there to highlight what is presented in the class and thereby gain excellent public speaking experience.

The parents will particularly enjoy the presentation. Students tend to be live wires, yet articulate, when given this task. The parents of the children making the presentation will, of course, be very proud of their offspring.

You will have to be in the classroom to answer any questions directed at you but, all in all, you, as the teacher, will be pleasantly surprised at how well the students can describe a facet of your material. A certain amount of precoaching is required, of course, but you will find it very worthwhile on almost every front.

© 1996 by The Center for Applied Research in Education

67. MISSIONS POSSIBLE

Problem: You are looking for a knowledgeable guest speaker to come to your History or Social Studies class to speak about a foreign country. Where can you get such a resource person readily available in your community for no or low cost?

Solution: A large number of churches in the communities across North America have sent missionaries throughout the world. Many of these missions people retired and returned home from the mission field. In most cases, part of being a missionary is being a professional, so for the most part these people would have experience talking to different groups.

You will find that these former missionaries are more than willing to come to talk to your students about the country where they served God.

A phone call to the clergyperson at a local church will get you the names of several former or retired missionaries. It has been my experience with these people to find that they are highly motivated with excellent person skills. They, as a rule, are very good at answering questions from the students and have good descriptive techniques.

The former missionary will often have a series of slides or artifacts from the country they worked in. This greatly adds to the educational value of their presentation.

The retired missions field worker is a strong, reliable asset to your classroom. The descriptions and feelings of a person who has worked in a foreign culture are of immense educational value.

68. THE END-OF-THE-YEAR BOOK

Problem: You would like to have something from each class to help you remember the joys and sorrows as the years go by. You would like the students to be able to recall their year with you in a positive way.

The school yearbook is good in itself, but it shows precious little about your individual class and it certainly doesn't focus on the day-to-day situations and peculiarities that you encounter.

What can you do to help remember your school years? What can you create with the students that will be a worthwhile memento of your year with them?

Solution: Make an end-of-the-year book or booklet. This booklet would contain happenings from the year compiled by you and the students.

There are a couple of keys to preparing this booklet that will minimize your organizational problems of collecting information.

The first key is to reduce your extra workload on this by making the project into an English or History/Social Studies/Civics/Psychology or Language Arts assignment for the students.

When explaining the assignment, tell the students they are to describe the positive or fun things and the negative or problem things that happened to them during each week. Students are to be precise and truthful. Each student is to make at least one contribution every week. This process is important because it is necessary to include something from each student in the year-end booklet.

At the end of each week or time period, the data collected is graded, then added to and edited by you or a designated student. When you reach the end of the school year, the happenings are combined and placed in the end-of-the-year booklet.

The second way to collect data for your year-end booklet is to have a couple or three of the more aggressive students give a weekly record of the happenings to you. You can add your comments to their ideas ensuring that every student in the class is mentioned.

It is not a good idea to leave events longer than one week before collecting them because the number of things that happen around a school in a five-day period often equals a year's experience anywhere else.

© 1996 by The Center for Applied Research in Education

69. CLASS NAME PUZZLE

Problem: You are looking for a neat way for the new students to get to know each other's name at the start of a new school year.

Solution: Make a word puzzle using the students' names in the class. In order to do this, you need to use the open puzzle form (Figure 4–3).

With this form you write the first (and/or last) names of each student in the spaces and then write those names somewhere on the puzzle itself. After the names are in place, fill in the remaining blanks with letters of the alphabet.

Students will be delighted to work on this puzzle because they will look for their own names as well as their friends' names first, and then they will search out the names of the other students in the class.

This is a great way to teach everyone's name to all the students on the first days of a new year, or it can be used in the middle of the year as a fun event.

© 1996 by The Center for Applied Research in Education

(Figure 4–3)

OPEN PUZZLE FORM

Search for your name and your classmates' names.

Students' Names

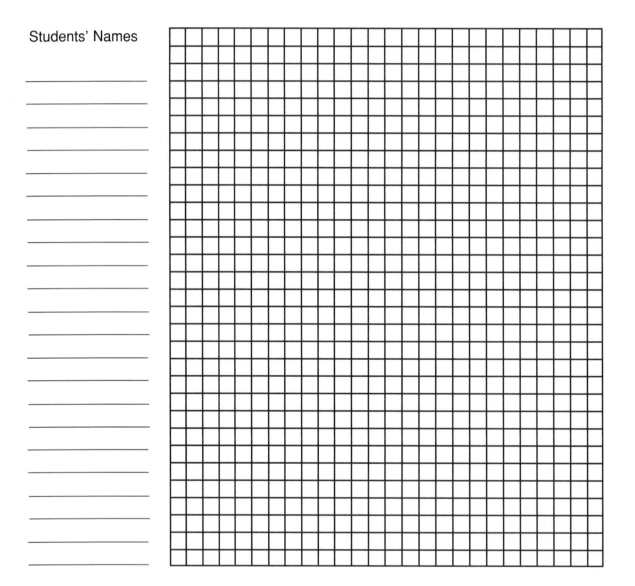

70. THE FOOD INGREDIENTS GAME (FIG)

Problem: Students eat junk food. In your Health class you want students to become aware of the things they are putting into their bodies.

How do you teach students in an interesting way about the contents of foods? How can you get students to read the labels on manufactured food products? What is the greatest amount of fun you will ever have teaching a class on nutrition?

Solution: Play the Food Ingredients Game (FIG). In this game, the teacher reads the lists of ingredients for nine well-known manufactured food products. The students are to guess from the ingredients the name or type of product the teacher is talking about. After the students have numbered their papers from one to nine, you, the teacher, read out all nine sets of ingredients, leaving enough time between each one for the students to jot down their answer. As soon as the students have finished writing down their guess for the last one, you then read number one again and ask the students what they think the correct answer would be. Write all the responses on the blackboard. At this point reveal the name for product number one by writing it beside the student responses. You then proceed to do the same for number two and so on until you have finished all nine.

The variety of responses will amaze you as well as the students. Most students will not properly connect the food names or brand names with the ingredient descriptions of the products. This process in itself will cause the student to be more aware of the contents of manufactured foods.

An excellent follow-up to this exercise is to ask the students a week or two later if they find themselves consciously or unconsciously reading the labels on the food products they see at home or in the grocery store.

FIG Ingredient List: Prior to reading the lists of ingredients to the students, tell them that in many countries the ingredients are listed on the label in descending order by amount. If sugar is listed first, then there is more sugar in the product than any other single item. There is not necessarily more sugar in the product than all the other ingredients put together.

1. Specially selected potatoes, hydrogenated vegetable oil, seasoning (sodium acetate, lactose, dextrose, malic acid), salt.

    Answer: Salt & Vinegar Potato Chips

2. Corn syrup solids, coconut oil, sodium caseinate, mono- and diglycerides, potassium phosphate, dibasic, sodium aluminum silicate, lactic acid, artificial flavors, acetic acid and color.

    Answer: Coffee creamer or whitener

3. Ground corn treated with calcium hydroxide, partially hydrogenated soybean oil, water and salt.

    Water, tomato paste, diced green chilies, salt, dehydrated onions, modified food starch, sugar, citric acid, onion powder, garlic powder.

    Dextrose, salt, corn flour, ground chilies, onion powder, cumin, garlic powder, citric acid, partially hydrogenated soybean oil, oregano, silicon dioxide added as an anti-caking agent.

    Answer: Taco Shell, Seasoning and Sauce Kit

4. Pork, water, salt, sugar, sodium phosphate, sodium nitrate, sodium erythorbate, smoke.

    Answer: Bacon

5. Milk, cream milk, liquid sugar, whey powder, corn syrup solids, cocoa powder, marshmallow (contains water, sugar, glucose, dextrose, modified starch, salt, citric acid, potassium sorbate, sodium benzoate, artificial flavor, color), almonds, chocolate (contains sugar, chocolate liquor, cocoa butter, soy lecithin), malt extract, mono- and diglycerides, locust bean gum, cellulose gum, guar gum, carrageenin, artificial flavor.

    Answer: Heavenly Hash Ice Cream

6. Sugar, dextrose, citric acid, trisodium citrate, natural flavor (contains BHA—a preservative), gum arabic, tricalcium phosphate, artificial flavor, maringin, vegetable shortening, vitamin C (214 mg per 100 g), food color.

    Answer: Orange Flavor Crystals

7. Vegetable oil, water, sugar, relish, white vinegar, tomato paste, salt, frozen yolk, xanthin gum, propylene glycol alginate, calcium disodium EDTA, color.

    Answer: Thousand Island Salad Dressing

8. Carbonated water, sugar, caramel color, phosphoric acid, natural flavors, caffeine.

    Answer: The Leading Cola Beverage

9. Dehydrated onions, salt, dextrose, hydrolyzed plant protein, dehydrated beef bone stock, sodium citrate, potato flour, yeast extract, vegetable oil, corn starch, caramel, potato starch, hydrogenated vegetable shortening (may contain palm oil), monosodium glutamate, disodium guanylate, and disodium inosinate.

    Answer: Onion Soup Mix

71. THE BOOK EXCHANGE TOKEN PROGRAM

Problem: You want to develop reading in your whole school. You would like to develop good P.R. with the community and have your school seen as a learning center that reaches out to the larger community.

You realize that not all people can afford to purchase books on a weekly basis.

How can you stimulate reading and book circulation within your school and your school's community?

Solution: Develop the Book Exchange Token Program with the students in your school. This essentially is a book fair that would normally occur on Friday afternoon of each week.

To develop the program you must tell the students that they are to bring a suitable reading book of any kind to the school. Students are to bring books that they have around the house and that no one is reading or likely to read in the near future (not their parent's expensive encyclopedias).

When a student brings a book to the collection person (usually the librarian), the student then receives a token worth one book. The collection person puts the books in boxes until Friday afternoon when they are then put on display in a large area such as the school gym.

The students with the tokens are then allowed to go to the Friday book fair to exchange their tokens for books they have not read and that are new to them.

The exchange can be developed to enable those students who did not bring a book to get a purchase token. Students in the school would be able to earn tokens by performing well in school work or in the school environment. The tokens would, therefore, become incentives for doing the ongoing tasks of the school.

If the program is developed to include all students, it becomes necessary for the collection person to become more aggressive and seek out book donations from the community at large. A small ad in the local newspaper will usually get the school an overabundance of appropriate books for the book exchange.

This idea has a multifold ripple effect in the community of the school. Not only are you bringing valuable used books back into the community, you are providing that reading material on a continuous basis at no cost to the student. The P.R. value of this idea is immeasurable. Everyone loves a good idea that works well and costs nothing.

72. THE "WELCOME BACK" BOOKLET

Problem: Your experience has told you that the first day of school can be somewhat of an organizational nightmare. Among other things, there is the collection of fees, the distribution of textbooks, the assigning of desks and the organization of an attendance system. There often is very little teaching this day because of these circumstances. This presents you with a problem in that, as you are collecting fees and organizing, what do you do with the new pupils sitting in the desks in front of you? You can't give them an assignment based on previous work with you because you never had them before. You do not know what personalities and skill levels are out there, so you must avoid assigning work that may be beyond the abilities of some students. What do you do to keep the students occupied while doing the organization on the first day?

Solution: Prepare a "Welcome Back" Booklet for the students to work on. This booklet would normally include low to medium skills but high interest materials.

Items that could be included in this booklet are:

* crossword puzzles
* word searches
* word games
* a basic math sheet (could be a skill-level indicator)
* mazes
* a coloring page
* a hidden objects page

The "Welcome Back" Booklet will help the students be on task right away on a nonthreatening bit of work. Most everyone will have a sense of accomplishment. This will help set the mood for the class.

© 1996 by The Center for Applied Research in Education

73. BEFORE-SCHOOL HAPPY GRAM

Problem: You want to start your school year off on the right foot with your primary students. You realize there can be much apprehension at this time as students get a "new" teacher. You recognize it is good P.R. to alleviate some of these anxieties a few days before school starts.

What is the best P.R. stress-reducing tool to use before the first day of classes?

Solution: Send a Before-School Happy Gram (Figure 4–4) to all the students on your class list. This Happy Gram is designed to make the incoming student feel warm fuzzies when he or she first greets you.

The parents of the child receiving the Before-School Happy Gram will feel terrific about this letter. It sets the mood for the year and tells the parents you are a positive happy person who believes in open communication with them and their child.

(Figure 4–4)

Before-School Happy Gram

THE TEDDY BEAR NAME TAG

I AM

School starts in a very few days. I am excited and can hardly wait to meet you. If you want, you may bring a teddy bear on the first day.

Would you please color and cut out the teddy bear name tag and put your name on it. We will all be wearing our name tags to school on the first day. I'll see you soon.

_____

Your Teacher this Year

74. LAS VEGAS MATH

Problem: How can you make math exciting? How can you cause students to look forward to being in your math group? In what way can you get students to rush to your class?

Solution: Make math class a game of chance. This idea will impart a little old-fashioned fun into your lessons.

Get a deck of playing cards or simply cut a series of cards from a piece of medium thick cardboard. The number of cards cut will be at your discretion. You may want to have exactly the number of cards as there are students in your class or you may want to have several more to increase the odds either way. You place these cards in a small jar or box on your desk or other convenient spot in the classroom.

On most of the cards you print "REGULAR ASSIGNMENT" but on one or more of the cards you print the word "FREE." If a student draws the free card, then that student either does not have to do the assignment or will have to do a reduced amount of work for that particular period.

On one or more cards you may want to write "OOPS!" The student who draws this card must do twice as much or an increased amount of work.

When the cards are returned, you must shuffle them so they are ready for the next class.

It is best to make Las Vegas Math optional because there are always those people who feel that any form of gambling is not the right thing to do and, of course, it is best to respect this.

Las Vegas Math will definitely stimulate interest and make the students want to come to class to draw their card for the day.

Las Vegas Math will maintain high interest because of the sporadic reinforcement that is built into the idea. Psychologists tell us that sporadic positive reinforcement builds commitment and causes people to have a higher desire to do something more often.

75. THE ROTATING "TEACHER'S PET" SYSTEM

Problem: Teachers can spot dependable students. There are usually one or two students who you can count on to run errands or do odd jobs. The students are usually reliable, aggressive and bright. You know these students will get extra tasks completed with a minimum of hassle. How do you avoid favoritism and spread the tasks consistently throughout the class?

Solution: Make every student a teacher's pet in turn. Put the name of every student in the class on a 2" × 6" piece of paper. Using a stiff piece of cardboard or by making a display on the bulletin board, create a "Teacher's Pet of the Week" sign. Leave room on the display for you to place three pockets (a cut-down envelope will do). On one pocket you print "Student Names" and on the other two pockets you print "TP1" or "TP2" respectively.

At the start of each week choose two new students to be the teacher's pets for that week. The grouping is at your discretion and should be designed such that you rotate through the whole class two or more times a year. When you need a person to run an errand or do a particular job, you choose one of the people whose names are in TP1 or TP2.

The main reason for having a TP1 and a TP2 is the fact that some students are not so reliable as others. You can group a strong TP1, for example, with a weak TP2. The stronger student will help the weaker one get a task accomplished for you. In the event you have a serious problem and you need only a good performer to do the job, you simply choose the more dependable of the two students to do the job.

This rotating "teacher's pet" system gives you control and allows students who would not normally be asked to do anything the opportunity to learn some sense of responsibility by performing needed tasks.

A secondary or added feature of this idea is the fact that you will never be accused of having a single teacher's pet again because you have a class full of them.

© 1996 by The Center for Applied Research in Education

76. READ A TUB TUB

Problem: You are looking for a unique reading center—a place where the kids will want to be and will want to read while there. Many teachers, especially at the grades one to three level, are looking for innovative ideas that will cause their students to have a desire to read on their own. The reading center must be a high-interest area that has a built-in behavior control mechanism.

Solution: For this idea you need an old-fashioned cast iron bath tub, the kind that has four legs protruding from the bottom.

The first thing you do is remove the taps and other related paraphernalia from the inside and from the outside of the bath tub.

You then have the option of painting the tub yourself (using oil-based paints), leaving the porcelain white, or giving your students a few brushes and letting them go to town.

Once the paint is thoroughly dry and a couple of fluffy pillows are tossed in, you are ready to proceed with your Read a Tub Tub Reading Center.

The basic instructions for the tub are as follows:

1. Students are allowed to go into the tub after they have successfully finished their school assignments.

2. There must be no attempt to tip the tub. You can stabilize the base of the tub by: (a) bolting the four legs to a piece of $4 \times 8 \times 3/4$ inch plywood and covering the plywood with rug; or (b) bolting the tub to the floor.

3. The tub is for reading only. This is the only activity allowed.

I said there must be a built-in control mechanism. This goes as follows: in order to control the number of students in the tub at one time, you need to make tub tickets. Students can sit in the tub to read if they have a tub ticket. You make a maximum of three tub tickets. Anyone not in possession of a tub ticket is not allowed in the tub.

Tub tickets must be earned. Finishing work successfully or doing some special task might earn a student a tub ticket. The criteria to earn a tub ticket is at your discretion.

77. ARGUMENTS

Problem: Many times a student will put an answer on one of your tests that is not right. However, from the point of view of the student (and others) he or she is correct in the response. An argument can be made that the answer, while not the right response you needed, is still technically correct. Many students will go away feeling cheated or at least frustrated because they "knew" their answer on the test was valid; however, you marked it as a wrong answer. How can you turn this situation into a learning experience for the student and in doing so, alleviate the sense of animosity the person feels over having his or her "right" answer marked as wrong? How can you get the students to do further research in your subject area and thereby reinforce the learning of your information?

Solution: Allow the students to give you a written argument describing in what way their answer on the test was the appropriate response to the question. Students are to describe in detail how their wrong answer was technically correct from their perspective. In this process, students are encouraged to do research in order to support their answer.

When a student presents you with a valid and strong argument supporting his or her answer, you then give the student all or part of the marks that would have been normally given for that question had the student given the correct answer in the first place.

It is best to limit arguments to only two questions per test; otherwise, some students would argue every question on every test, thus distorting the reason for the test in the first place.

There are three distinct advantages in allowing students to argue questions on a test.

1. Students will often work harder trying to prove the validity of their test answer than they did studying for the test in the first place. You therefore reinforce the learning of the original material.

2. The student is no longer apt to go home with the complaint that the teacher was "unfair" or that he or she was marked wrong for a completely right answer.

3. It gives the student some power to control or upgrade his or her mark.

It is true that some students will try to prove anything; therefore, you can expect some highly imaginative and creative arguments.

78. HOW TO GET PEN PALS IN A FOREIGN COUNTRY

Problem: I want to access foreign countries with my English class. I want to find pen pals (friends) in foreign lands. How do I get a letter to a classroom in another country so they can reply to us?

Solution: Have your students write a letter that describes their likes, wants and lifestyle. The letter should include probing questions about that foreign country the letter is going to. The questions will help elicit a response and you therefore give the people in the foreign country a basis for corresponding.

You should state that you "like" their country and need some information on that society. These ideas will help you get a better quality reply.

The key to accessing a classroom in another country is not in the development of the letter but rather in the creation of the address on the envelope and the actual destination of that envelope.

The destination of that envelope is all important because it must work for you on its own in that foreign country. You must therefore send the letter to a smaller town in that country of choice; some place where you can figure from your atlas that the population of the town is under 25,000 people. In other words, you want to send your letter to a town where the postmaster will likely know the name of the schoolmaster or of a school to forward your letter to. If you send your letter to a large center such as Paris or London, there is a good chance of your letter ending up in the "jolly ol' wastebin." It is not likely postal workers in a large city will have the circumstance to forward your letter to a school.

Your envelope should look something like the example here. The information is clear and specific.

To a Grade 8 level classroom
Any school (please forward)
Rochefort, France

You can improve your chance for success by supplying the postal code, which your own post office can supply.

© 1996 by The Center for Applied Research in Education

79. THE BUDGET GAME

Problem: You want to teach a totally practical lesson to your students about the cost of living. You would like your students to be aware of the difference between buying what you want and paying for what you need.

Many students in our society receive no information as to the cost of running a home. They simply let their parents pay the bills. They never need to know what things like groceries and utilities cost. These same students are suddenly faced with the shock of reality when it comes to living on their own. They then have to budget their incomes to face the never-before-seen demands of a water bill.

How can you develop economic understanding in your students that will help prepare them for the real world of personal financial accountability?

Solution: Play the Budget Game with the students. The game consists of a playing board (Figure 4–5) which lists a series of genuine needs that are necessary to run an average household for a single month. Included on this board are a series of unnecessary wants that the students have an equal opportunity to spend their money on.

You, as the teacher, would write on the blackboard the approximate average monthly income for your area. You then read to the students the following guidelines:

1. They are to spend their "incomes" judiciously on the items they feel are important for the month. They are to estimate the cost of each item.

2. Students do not have to spend money on every item on the board.

3. Students do not have to spend all of the money.

There are basically two ways of playing the game once the students know the average income.

The first way is to copy the budget game board we provide and have the students work individually or in groups of not more than three. In this case, they are to write the amount spent on each item directly on the photocopied sheet.

The second way is to transfer the data onto large sheets of stiff cardboard. In this situation, the teacher can have larger groups working on a single board. With larger groups, roles can be assigned, such as parents, sisters, brothers, even an extended relative or two. Students would then be asked to make the economic demands on the family that would be suitable for their role.

The larger boards would require the teacher to provide a number of slips of paper for students to write their purchase amounts on. This would prevent students from writing on your Budget Game board.

Once the students have all made their choices as to where to spend their hard-earned cash, you, as the teacher, present to them the *ideal* spending pattern for the amount of money they have.

© 1996 by The Center for Applied Research in Education

You then go through each item one at a time. It is their degree of deviation from this ideal spending pattern that will reveal how realistic the students are. This indeed is where the "teachable moment" occurs. While students are arguing vehemently that fifty dollars a month for groceries is sufficient and that it is a necessity to spend thirty-five dollars on candy, you can inject the reality of what it costs their parents to feed, house and clothe them. In all likelihood, the money spent by their parents is probably not far from the ideal that you have displayed.

If you so desire, you can expand the Budget Game by saying, after the game appears to have finished, that Aunt Erna has died in Boise, and it will cost your budget $300.00 or more to go to the funeral. Tell the students that decisions are to be made. They must go back to the budget board and find the necessary funds to go to the funeral. This has to be done by cutting items and paring down others. Ask the students what logic can be applied (for example, they will need less groceries at home because they will be at the funeral for a period of time).

Once the students have completed a session or two with the Budget Game, they will see some light at the end of the real-world tunnel. They will have a much better understanding of what lies ahead for them, as well as gain a greater appreciation of what their parents must put out each month.

BUDGET GAME SHEET

(Figure 4-5)

Groceries	Candy	Go to Circus	Power (Gas/Light)	Paint the House	New Bike	School Supplies
$ _____	$ _____	$ 100.00	$ _____	$ _____	$ _____	$ _____ /month
Cat Food	Electronic Game	Rent/Mortgage	New Rug	Car Payment	Automobile Fuel/Oil	Automobile Repair
$20.00	$ _____	$ _____	$ _____	$207.00	$ _____	$75.00
Registration Volleyball	Clothes	Eat at Fast-Food Restaurant	Scout Dues	Cable T.V.	Hobby	Make-up
$10.00 per member	$ _____	$ _____	$ _____	$ _____	$20.00	$ _____
Party	Beauty Parlor	Newspaper	Birthday Gift (for friend)	House Taxes & Insurance	Loan Sister	Water Bill
$ _____	$ _____	$ _____	$ _____	$ _____	$ _____	$ _____
$110.00	Diamond Ring	House Repair (roof leaks)	Pay Back Loan	School Fees	New Skates or Skis	Phone Bill
Movies	$ _____	$ _____	$40.00	$ _____	$35.00	$ _____
$ _____						

80. THE AFTER-ASSIGNMENT ENJOYMENT BOOKLET

Problem: Some students finish their school assignments before others. When you give an assignment to the class as a whole, you will be faced with the fact that students' skills vary to a large extent. Some students will take to the assignment with vigor and complete the work before the period is finished. Others may have the same degree of enthusiasm, but it may take them the whole period to complete the task.

What do you do with those students who finish early? How do you keep these early finishers from becoming bored or disruptive?

Solution: Provide an "After-Assignment Enjoyment Booklet" for the students to work with.

This booklet is to be created by you, usually on a weekly basis. It would normally contain things that the students like to do, such as word find games, dot to dot, coloring pages and so forth. Even a blank page or two for doodling would be useful.

Remember, this booklet is to function for you, the teacher. Care is to be taken to make sure students do not rush through their regular assignments in order to do the Enjoyment Booklet.

This After-Assignment Enjoyment Booklet can, in itself, be used as an educational tool. Many word find sheets are excellent spelling reinforcers. Crossword puzzles can be seen as studies in word usage. You can intellectually challenge your students with this idea and even target certain skills if you so desire. It all depends on the type of material you choose to place in the booklet.

81. SPLAT! PUNCTUATION SYSTEM

Problem: You want your students to understand the need for and the use of punctuation marks. You are looking for a novel way for students to remember where the punctuation marks go.

What is a truly interesting way to teach punctuation skills?

Solution: Sound out the punctuation as you make hand gestures.

With this idea, each different punctuation mark would have a different sound and a different gesture. For example, a period would consist of a straight forward point of the index finger, as you say the word, "Splat."

The following is a list of punctuation marks and a description of the gestures used to help describe them.

Period . One point of the index finger while saying the word, "splat."

Colon : Two points of the index finger, one on top of the other, and the expression, "splat, splat."

Exclamation Point ! One long downward movement of the arm, with a point of the index finger at the bottom. The sound would be "whoosh," as your arm goes down, and "splat," as you point with the index finger.

Question Mark ? One round swirl of your hand with a straight line at the bottom after the swirl, then a point of the index finger at the bottom. The sound would be "zowie," as you make the swirl, and "splat," as you point with the index finger at the bottom.

Apostrophe ' This is made with a twist of two fingers together in the air as you say, "eek."

Hyphen - Raise your right arm about chest height and swing it quickly in front of you in one strong swift motion. The sound as you do this is "whap."

Comma , This is made with the arm sticking straight out in front of you, and with a closed fist, you give your wrist a twist as you say, "glitz."

Semi Colon ; This is made by a direct point of the index finger and the word, "splat," followed by a twist of the wrist with the closed fist as you say, "glitz."

Quotation Marks " " Raise both hands about ear height on either side of you and move the index finger and the middle finger on each hand in a small up and down motion as you say, "quote, quote."

This unique presentation of the different forms of punctuation will continue to reinforce learning as you read a paragraph that is full of examples. It will be a gesture and sound extravaganza.

You will definitely enjoy this presentation to the students as they learn these aspects of English.

© 1996 by The Center for Applied Research in Education

82. IT'S A PET OF AN IDEA

Problem: You are looking for a way to teach basic skills, such as responsibility, care for the environment, cleanliness, and so forth, to your kindergarten or grade one students.

Solution: Bring a pet to live in the class. Many teachers have animals that live quite nice lives among the children in the classroom. There are some considerations to be aware of when you are thinking of bringing a pet into the classroom:

1. Some students may be allergic to the odors or the fur of some animals.

2. Some school boards have a written policy concerning pets in the classroom. Check this out.

3. You must contact your school board and teacher's association to see if there has been any litigation in this area that would affect the placing of an animal in your classroom.

4. Your branch of the S.P.C.A. will have regulations that need to be adhered to.

5. Any animal, whether in an enclosed structure (terrarium) or not, must be of a benign nature.

6. Normally the animal must remain in the confines of the classroom and not be able to wander in the school.

7. The animal must be able to sustain a certain amount of person contact.

8. Stay away from exotic animals, even if they are donated to you.

9. Provision must be made for the care of the animal while school is not in session.

The pet in the classroom will teach responsibility in terms of feeding and general care of an animal. Regular duties can be assigned to different students on a rotational basis, so all students can share the responsibilities.

Many students do not have the home situation wherein they can have a pet of their own. The animal you have in the class will open students' eyes as to the amount and type of care that is required to keep a pet.

It is of paramount importance that the students and the animal are protected at all times. The children should be taught safe and proper handling, feeding and clean-up procedures before the animal arrives.

The benefits of having a pet in the classroom far outweigh the problems associated with it. You will see growth in the areas of caring and compassion in your students as they learn to be responsible for the animal in their midst.

83. COOL SPELLING

Problem: It is wintertime, and you are teaching somewhere north of Provo, Utah or Columbus, Ohio, and there is snow on the ground. You are looking for a novel way to reinforce spelling skills in your elementary students.

How can you practice spelling outside when snow covers the school yard?

Solution: Have the students write the words from the spelling assignment in large letters in the snow. This is accomplished by gathering a quantity of squeezable ketchup or shampoo bottles. You then mix enough warm water and food coloring to fill up the bottles. Once you have filled the bottles with bright colored water, take the students outside and give them a demonstration on how to use the squeezable bottles as a writing instrument in the snow.

There are three guidelines for this activity:

1. Students are to avoid getting the colored water on their clothing (gloves or mittens) or hands.

2. Students are to work in pairs so one of the two can check for correctness.

3. Students are to dress appropriately for the climate outside.

84. HOW TO PLAY "BOOM BAH" IN THE CLASSROOM

Problem: You want to enhance eye-to-hand skills in your students. You would like to stimulate motor development in order to help with keyboarding or any other eye-to-hand coordination skill.

How do you teach a motor skill that involves the use of sight directly influencing hand motions?

Solution: Play the game of Boom Bah in the classroom. This is a hand signal game that strengthens speed and accuracy of eye-to-hand responses.

This game can be played by as few as five students or as many as thirty. Fifteen to twenty are ideal.

Students place their desks in a circle around the classroom. The teacher is the first leader to get the game going. Normally the teacher sits at a student desk. Every student at every desk is required to have a different hand signal. This signal may be anything from a thumbs-up sign, the peace sign or any one of a thousand derivations. A list of twenty signals is given at the end.

Once everyone, including the teacher, has their own hand signal and knows everybody else's, the teacher and the students begin to rhythmically slap their hands on the desks. The teacher then says to everyone, "What's the Name of the Game?," and all the students respond by saying, "Boom Bah." The teacher then starts the game off by doing his or her hand signal and then doing somebody else's hand signal. The person whose signal the teacher did must now do his or her own signal and do somebody else's signal, and that other person in turn does his or her hand signal and then does somebody else's. This continues in random order around the circle of twenty or so students until somebody makes a mistake in the pattern or is too slow to respond. The whole group then sings the following positive or upbeat line to that person, "We like___Bill___(student's name) Shish, Boom, Bah, Start the game, it's the Law." The person who made the error would then repeat what the teacher said in order to start the game. He or she would say, "What's the Name of the Game?" Everyone would again respond by saying, "Boom Bah." That person (Bill) would do his or her hand signal, then do someone else's, and so the game begins again until another person makes a mistake and the line is sung to somebody else and so on.

This hand signal game will get very loud as students slap their hands on the desk, and it can be very fast as students develop their skills of eye-to-hand coordination. Some warning should be given to neighboring classrooms before you begin Boom Bah, as the noise emitting from your class is bound to overflow.

Due to the nature of this game and the fact that a song is sung to the person who makes an error, it is best to explain this to the students first and that participation be optional, as some students may be unsure of the process. Once the game gets going and students see the genuine fun in Boom Bah, almost everyone will join in.

Here is a list of twenty hand signals that are great for Boom Bah.

★ Peace sign

★ Grab the nose

★ Pat top of the head

★ Touch ear lobe

★ One finger under chin

★ Hold three fingers up

★ Clasp hands together

★ Two thumbs up

★ Touch left or right arm with hand of other arm

★ Touch left or right shoulder with hand of other arm

★ Thumbs up

★ Thumbs down

★ Salute

★ Hold one finger up

★ Hold one finger down

★ One-finger point

★ Twiddle thumbs

★ Arm straight up in the air

★ Push away sign with one or two hands

★ One fist on top of another

Best Suited for
Grade 7 to Grade 9 (and Kindergarten)

85. THE CARE HELPER PROGRAM

Problem: You would like to provide some unusual enrichment for your junior high students. You would like your students to develop compassion and reliability through responsibility.

Where in the school system can students learn to be altruistic through interaction?

Solution: Develop the Care Helper Program between the kindergarten or grade one class and your junior high classroom. With this program those junior high students who are judged to be capable of learning by helping would become Care Helpers in a grade one or kindergarten classroom. These would be students capable of keeping up with their assignments through regular or special arrangements.

Once parents, administration and students have been informed of the Care Helper Program, you would need to set up a working schedule with the kindergarten or grade one teachers.

The Care Helper Program has been more than successful throughout North America. There are a number of important benefits for all the people concerned. Some of these are:

1. The kindergarten and grade one students will have a strong role model from which to learn physical and social skills.

2. The junior high students can learn by helping. These students will have excellent growth in almost every skill area as they are given some responsibility.

3. The kindergarten or grade one teacher will appreciate the extra set of capable hands to help perform the billion or so tasks associated with a kindergarten or grade one classroom.

4. Care Helpers are very enthusiastic and helpful when working with special needs or handicapped children.

5. Care Helpers are a definite asset when the younger students are taken on field trips. They assist the teacher in organizing and keeping track of the many details associated with taking the younger students on an outing.

The Care Helper Program is a no-cost program that produces meaningful results because the students gain at every level. Compassion and reliability are learned through responsibility.

86. THE ENERGETIC THREE-CHAIRED DATA REVIEW GAME

Problem: You are looking for an exciting information review game. You want to provide a highly stimulating learning situation for your students. Noise is no barrier this time.

How can you get everyone excited about the chapter review? How can you get one hundred percent attention for the duration of the review session?

Solution: Play "The Energetic Three-Chaired Data Review Game."

This game requires you to have prepared a list of review questions. You will present these either verbally or by way of an overhead projector.

The game is set up by having the students sitting in pairs in a circle around the classroom with an extra or empty chair beside each pair of students. This means that for every pair of students you would have three chairs. Each chair group of three should be numbered in chronological order.

Chair group number one is the only group that would have all three chairs occupied by students as you start the game.

The next step is to begin asking your review questions of the three students in group number one. Because the students are in competition with one another, they should be encouraged to blurt out the answer. The student with the first correct answer can then move to the empty chair of pair group number two. You then move to the now three students in chair group number two and ask them a review question. The person who gets it correct first is allowed to move to the empty chair of group number three, and you then move to group number three and ask another review question, and so it goes.

The eventual winner of The Energetic Three-Chaired Data Review Game is the person who gets back to his or her original home group chair. It should be noted that this game can get a bit rambunctious as students blurt out answers and jostle chairs. Therefore, it may be advisable to forewarn colleagues in neighboring classrooms. This game is one of the most entertaining and rewarding ways to reinforce the learning of your material. You will notice that while pairs of students in the other chairs are not answering the questions, they are absorbing the review data. You, therefore, have direct learning as you specifically ask questions of students and you have vicarious learning as others listen in.

You may wish to use these same questions as a review test at some later date. The answers are more likely to be in place because of The Energetic Three-Chaired Data Review Game.

© 1996 by The Center for Applied Research in Education

87. THE UP, DOWN AND SIDEWAYS PUZZLE

Problem: You need a twenty-minute enjoyable reinforcer for the data in your subject area. You would like this to be a game that is rewarding to the extent that students will "ask" to play.

What exercise or game needs no preparation and will enhance the students' knowledge of the vocabulary in your targeted subject area?

Solution: Have the students do the Up, Down and Sideways Puzzle on the inventory of words associated with your subject. In this puzzle, students are to spell different words and *match* letters as they are written vertically and horizontally on the grid.

Points may be given toward a prize if the students are able to match two, three or even four letters vertically and horizontally.

The reproducible Up, Down and Sideways Puzzle form (Figure 4–6) is provided for your convenience.

(Figure 4–6)

THE UP, DOWN AND SIDEWAYS PUZZLE FORM

Write the words vertically and horizontally, matching up as many letters as possible. Use 26 words.

Name: _____   Subject Area: _____

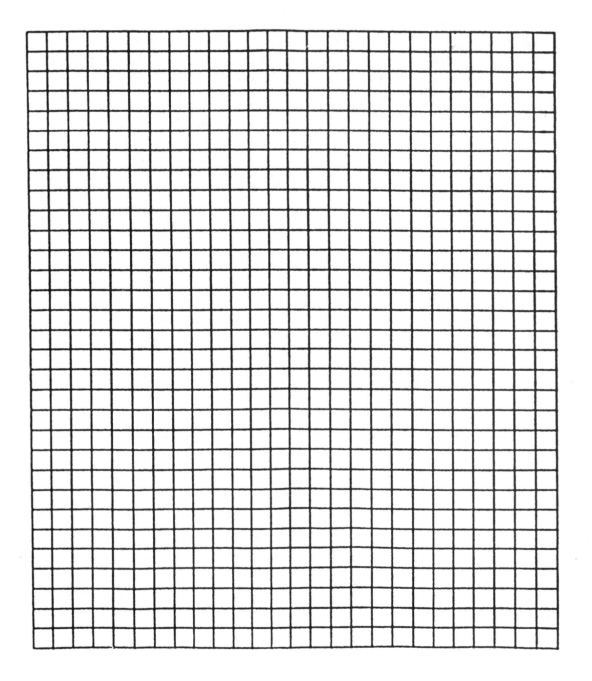

88. SUBJECT BINGO

Problem: You are teaching a class that contains a good number of symbols and terms. Subjects like music or science are typical. You are searching for a high-interest teaching idea that will lead to a large degree of understanding of the data you present.

How can you reinforce the learning of symbols, terms and definitions in a way that leads to strong retention?

Solution: Introduce the subject bingo game.

Once you have introduced or covered seventy-five or more terms and symbols in a subject like music, you will be ready to proceed with your music bingo game.

Follow these procedures:

1. Make your bingo cards from laminated stiff cardboard (Figure 4–7).
2. Place the twenty-four terms or symbols on the cards in such a way that no two cards are exactly the same.
3. Make about four more cards than you have students.
4. Play the bingo game by reading out the definitions or by describing the symbol picked from a hat or box.
5. Have a master sheet on which to place your called-out symbols or definitions.
6. It is up to you whether or not you want to provide small prizes for the winners. You will find that the game is rewarding in itself.

Once you have played several bingo games, a forty- or fifty-term test would be a natural outcome of the bingo sessions.

(Figure 4–7)

SAMPLE BINGO CARD

This is what a typical subject BINGO card should look like.

M	U	S	I	C
♩	♯	*p*	𝄞	Allegro
𝅝	♮	*mf*	≡	Crescendo
♪	♭	FREE	𝄢	Vivace
♩		*ff*	‖:∷‖	Bass
♪	⌣	*pp*	▭	Soprano

★ 5 ★

COMMUNICATION AND PROFESSIONAL IDEAS

Some concepts do not directly apply to students, but they are highly important to the teaching staff.

Communication and Professional Ideas targets those concepts that aid you in your workaday world of colleagues, parents and students. Using the tools contained in this section, such as communication with administration and survival and success guidelines for parent-teacher conferences, will make your teaching time more efficient and rewarding.

89. SURVIVAL AND SUCCESS GUIDELINES FOR PARENT-TEACHER CONFERENCES

Problem: The main reason for having the parent-teacher conference is to discuss the academic and social performance of students. You, as the teacher, want this process to be as smooth and informative as possible. If you look at the dynamics of any classroom, you can see the potential for some of those conferences not being smooth. Added to this is the variability of parents—some you may perceive as aggressive and others benign with most falling somewhere in the middle.

How can you promote successful parent-teacher conferences that allow for a maximum of exchange of information and a minimum of stress?

Solution: Be prepared! A state of readiness is always your first line of defense. In order to help you prepare, read the following set of guidelines:

1. Interview each student a few days ahead of the conference. Discuss the student's strengths and weaknesses and make notes.

2. Send a memo or letter home to inform the parents of the times and location of the conference or interview.

3. Use the Parent-Teacher Conference Checklist of Skills (Figure 5–1), as a discussion paper from which speak. This checklist should be prepared by you before the conference takes place. Ideally this checklist should be combined with the student's report card or grades when talking to the parents. However, it can be used if parent-teacher conferences are held before the first set of grades or report cards come out.

4. Begin the conference with a positive statement about the child. This is a very important point. Speaking positively immediately about the child will quickly help to break down any misconceptions that may exist.

5. Have two or more different evaluation tools such as tests, essays and reports to show the parents how you derived the grade standing for their child. If you use only one test or essay for a term mark, you are leaving yourself open to a valid criticism. One score or grade for a term will not accurately tell you of the performance of a student.

6. Have a few examples of the student's work to show the parents. This is important as it will usually justify the grading level in which the child is placed.

7. Don't sit behind a monstrous desk to conduct your conferences or interviews. Sit at a separate table that is more open and less threatening.

8. Organize and clean your classroom if that is where the conference takes place.

9. Don't read your own press clippings. Some parents will tell you how totally wonderful you are. Don't let this go to your head.

10. When talking about a student's problem, tell the parents the exact details and consequences. Be specific. Make sure the problem and the resolution are described as tactfully as possible by you. Do not blame the parents for the behavior of their child.

11. Do not compare siblings.

12. Hone your listening skills. You will find that parents will have a lot to say about their children. They will often give you insights that will be invaluable to you when teaching their child.

13. Avoid arguments at all costs.

14. Do not run down a colleague. If a parent is angry about another teacher's behavior, do not participate in this even if you agree. It is not ethical to criticize a colleague.

15. Have a working knowledge of your school's programs outside your classroom. You may have to tap into a Cooperative Work Experience Class, for example, for one of your students. It is important for you to be able to describe these programs to parents at the conference should that become necessary.

16. Learn how to wrap up or close a conference. Most parents can sense when an interview or conference is over; however, some parents just won't stop talking about their child. If parents won't respond to subtle cues, you will simply have to tell them that their conference is over and others are waiting. If you can't do this, you run the risk of alienating a parent waiting at the door.

    Some teachers use a timer that will ring every fifteen or twenty minutes. However, this can be restrictive as some conferences by necessity need to go on longer.

17. Keep a list of the parents or guardians you talked to. This is important administrative data. You will no doubt be asked after the conference how many and which parents spoke to you. Use the Parent-Teacher Conference Record Sheet for this (Figure 5–2).

(Figure 5–1)

PARENT-TEACHER CONFERENCE CHECKLIST OF SKILLS

NAME: _____

Discussion Areas	Excellent	Good	Needs Support	Comments
Dependability – begins work when assigned				
– follows directions				
– completes tasks				
Independence – self starter; begins work without being told				
Honesty – tells truth				
– seeks permission				
– returns materials				
Communication Skills – with teachers				
– with peers				
– anger control				
Personal Appearance – student dresses appropriately				
– student is clean				
– neatly combed hair				

(Figure 5–2)

PARENT-TEACHER CONFERENCE RECORD SHEET

TEACHERS: To help us get an indication of the number of parents who came to Parent/ Teacher interviews, please fill out this sheet during your interviews and return it to the office after the interviews.

1. _____
2. _____
3. _____
4. _____
5. _____
6. _____
7. _____
8. _____
9. _____
10. _____
11. _____
12. _____
13. _____
14. _____
15. _____
16. _____
17. _____
18. _____
19. _____
20. _____

21. _____
22. _____
23. _____
24. _____
25. _____
26. _____
27. _____
28. _____
29. _____
30. _____
31. _____
32. _____
33. _____
34. _____
35. _____
36. _____
37. _____
38. _____
39. _____
40. _____

90. THE SUBSTITUTE TEACHER'S HANDBOOK

Problem: Substitute teachers are hired on a regular basis by almost all schools. Quite often that substitute teacher is new to the school and school system and therefore will be unaware of the many processes and idiosyncrasies of the school and the classroom he or she is to teach in.

How do you inform the substitute teacher of how your school functions? How do you help the substitute follow your methods of instruction while you are away?

Solution: Prepare a substitute teacher's handbook. This handbook will include those necessary items that pertain to the day-to-day routine of the school as well as those items that are important to individual classes.

This means that the handbook would have at least two sections. The first section would deal with school procedure such as: hall monitors, school rules, bell times and the length of periods. This section would normally be prepared by the central office of the school.

The second section of the handbook would be unique to individual classes. Items such as seating plans, classroom rules and use of work stations would be prepared by the classroom teachers.

In effect, each handbook would be different for each class. In this way, desires and expectations of individual teachers will be respected.

The substitute teacher's handbook helps the person replacing you do things your way. Instead of entering a classroom "cold turkey," the substitute would now have a better chance of performing his or her tasks without making some of those technical errors that can occur when a new person does not know the routine.

91. THE PRINCIPAL-TEACHER COMMUNICATION TOOL

Problem: You never see your school administrator except for staff meetings. You have little or no input into the overall function of the school. You have feelings of isolation and anomie (normlessness).

Principals and vice principals are extremely busy, so much so that there is often very little time in the course of a term to effectively communicate with staff members. This problem is especially acute in schools where the student population exceeds three hundred.

How can open communication be fostered in a school? How can principals and vice principals allow for a quality exchange of ideas with the people who teach and work with them?

Solution: Use the Principal-Teacher Communication Tool (Figure 5–3). This sheet lists eight areas of discussion that are important to the ongoing relationship between teachers in a school and the administration of that school.

The main thrust of this tool is to open and enhance communication between the principal and the teaching staff; therefore, it should be seen as being mutually beneficial to all parties concerned.

The greater the degree of open communication in a school or school system, the greater the harmony in that school or system. When teachers or staff have little or no input to the administration, they begin to feel like powerless pawns in the scheme of things.

The Principal-Teacher Communication Tool is designed to be nonthreatening, as well as to be highly efficient in gathering information. This tool should be given out to the staff members about a week to five days prior to the actual meeting. This will give the teachers a chance to think it over and be able to constructively communicate to the principal when the meeting occurs.

The principal or vice principal should schedule a block of time for the meetings when the Principal-Teacher Communication Tool is distributed. This will allow teachers to pick and choose the time when they are best able to attend.

© 1996 by The Center for Applied Research in Education

(Figure 5–3)

PRINCIPAL-TEACHER COMMUNICATION TOOL

Let's discuss . . . Please give these ideas some thought. I will see you on _____.

1. What are your professional teaching goals this year?

    _____

    _____

2. Which areas of teaching concern you? What would you like to change or improve?

    _____

    _____

3. Which procedures in our school are vague or could be improved upon?

    _____

    _____

4. Which areas of discipline are you strong in? How can we improve schoolwide discipline procedures?

    _____

    _____

5. From your perspective as a teacher, what is going well? What do you like?

    _____

    _____

6. What class level or subjects would you like to teach next term? What would you change from your present teaching load?

    _____

    _____

7. In terms of your professional career, where would you like to be next year?

    _____

    _____

8. How can the Principal and other members of the school office help you?

    _____

    _____

92. THE TEXT MONITOR SHEET

Problem: In many schools textbooks are given out to the students. Those textbooks are often paid for by the local or state educational authority and therefore must be kept in the best condition possible from year to year because textbook budgets are not overflowing at the best of times.

How do you, as a teacher, make the students responsible for the condition of their textbooks? How do you know what amount of damage is caused each year to specific textbooks and therefore be able to charge the students a fair and equitable amount of money for the misuse or abuse of those specific texts?

Solution: Give the students a Text Monitor Sheet (Figure 5–4). This sheet lists the name and number of the text along with a written description and a numerical rating of the text's condition. The quantity and type of marks or abuse on the text are to be described in as great a detail as possible by the student. The student then returns the Text Monitor Sheet to the teacher where that teacher makes an estimation of the number of years of service that would normally be remaining for the textbook. The average life expectancy of a textbook is five years. This may extend up to ten years if the use is nominal and the quality of the binding is very good.

With this Text Monitor Sheet the teacher has two sets of information that will be of tremendous benefit when students or their parents are charged for text misuse or abuse.

The student and the teacher agree on the data on the Text Monitor Sheet by virtue of their signatures. This agreement and information will in itself save wear and tear on texts as students will be conscious of the Text Monitor Sheet by which their books will be compared with at the end of the school year or term.

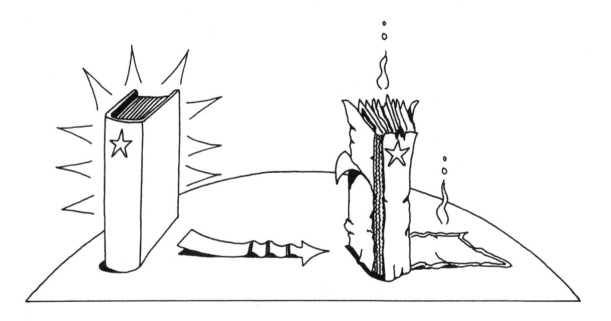

© 1996 by The Center for Applied Research in Education

(Figure 5–4)

TEXT MONITOR SHEET

YEAR _____   NAME _____

– –

SUBJECT/BOOK TITLE	BOOK NUMBER	BOOK'S CONDITION	
		BEFORE	AFTER
1. _____ Teacher estimate of number of years of service remaining for this text _____			
2. _____ Teacher estimate of number of years of service remaining for this text _____			
3. _____ Teacher estimate of number of years of service remaining for this text _____			
4. _____ Teacher estimate of number of years of service remaining for this text _____			
5. _____ Teacher estimate of number of years of service remaining for this text _____			
6. _____ Teacher estimate of number of years of service remaining for this text _____			
7. _____ Teacher estimate of number of years of service remaining for this text _____			

_____   _____
Student's Signature   Teacher's Signature

93. OBVIOUS TEACHING STRATEGIES AND THINGS YOU SHOULD ALREADY KNOW

Problem: How can you remember all those obvious little rules that are the bread and butter of teaching?

Solution: Keep the following list pinned up on your bulletin board or taped to your desk.

THINGS YOU SHOULD ALREADY KNOW BUT MAYBE FORGOT

1. When in doubt, don't. (When in doubt, be conservative.)
2. Have a locking filing cabinet.
3. Use timetable sheets for elementary math.
4. Try to avoid having the Christmas Pageant carved in stone.
5. Buy yourself a 3-hole punch.
6. Make friends with the janitor.
7. Attach your keys permanently to your body or place them on a large ring.
8. Count the students on and off the bus when going to and returning from field trips.
9. Do not give out nonprescription medications to any student at any time under any circumstances. Do not administer injections (e.g., for diabetics) at any time under any circumstances.
10. Employ the buddy system when taking younger students on field trips.
11. Talk to a colleague your own age.
12. Don't have more than four students working on a particular project at one time.
13. Read the staff notices.
14. Do not keep anything sharp or hot that is not locked up in your classroom.
15. Videotape yourself so you can improve your skills.
16. Let only one or two students go to the washrooms at a time.
17. Keep extra copies of texts in your classroom.
18. Do a "directions list" for each term. This tells you how many tests and assignments you need for your various classes and when they will be done.
19. Don't throw out that old typewriter even if you have a new word processor.
20. Instantly change the seating arrangement of your class if two or more students are talking or causing a disturbance.
21. Praise behavior, not personalities.
22. Remember that 90% of students will not perform tasks because they are afraid to fail.
23. Don't forget that students cannot predict very well.
24. If you don't know something, then admit it.

© 1996 by The Center for Applied Research in Education

25. Keep a box of tissues on your desk.

26. Tie a pen to your desk.

27. Keep an appointment book.

28. Keep a paper recycle box.

29. Use the broken record technique when students want to justify their poor behavior.

30. Allow zero tolerance for put-downs in your classroom.

31. Provide a wide range of topics when assigning a report so all the students won't be scrambling for a few resources.

32. Don't deny your spiritual self—go to a church or temple of your choice.

33. When students work on group projects, tell each student to initial the bottom right-hand corner of the pages he or she has worked on. This will tell you which students completed any part of the group project.

34. Don't be a pack rat; create "One of Everything" binders. Place one copy of everything you do in binders. Throw out or recycle the rest.

35. Keep a scrapbook(s) of your teaching career.

36. Join teacher interest groups.

37. Do not read the cumulative folders of a student until you have formed your own opinion of him or her.

38. Give positive nicknames to students.

39. Do ice breakers—walk into a fresh class and ask, "Who had a good weekend (day)?" This will set the mood for the day.

40. Take a cellular phone on field trips. The local phone company may donate one for the day.

41. Keep a box of crayons in your desk.

42. Give exact instructions in total detail to weaker students.

43. Keep extra clothing for yourself in a locked filing cabinet.

44. Keep a file of insta-work (crossword puzzles, word puzzles, and so forth) for those times you must cover a class for another teacher and you have been given no time to prepare.

45. When describing parameters of behavior, tell students, "This is what I am prepared to do and this is what I am prepared to live with."

46. At an awards assembly, if you have an excellent performing student who gets several awards, have one of the speakers praise the student's parents because of their consistent reliability.

47. Principals and administrators—keep an open box of candy on your desk.

48. Have a teacher-of-the-month profile and picture on the wall in a conspicuous space.

49. Do mad moments—give out fifty questions and see how many students can do in 60 seconds or 5 minutes or 10 minutes.

50. Tell the students who deserve it—"I trust you."

51. Make test prep work worth 5-10% of the test.

52. When a student asks why he or she has to do this or that, tell him or her "It's because I like you."

53. Have a CPR inservice for your staff.

54. Tell the excellent students "You are excellent."

55. Photocopy your mark/record book as you near the end of a term, semester or year.

94. THE THREE BASIC FORMS YOU NEED

Problem: You need certain basic forms to run a classroom. What are these forms and how do they help make your life easier?

Solution: There are three school forms that are important in almost every classroom. They help keep you organized and improve your efficiency in the areas of planning and recordkeeping.

The Seating Plan Form (Figure 5–5) Each classroom should have a seating plan that works for the teacher as well as the students. It will minimize the noise and related problems in the class if the students are seated continuously in the same desks.

It is often necessary to have certain personalities isolated from one another or there may be special needs such as eyesight problems that can be addressed by the positioning of students.

It is important for substitute teachers to be aware of the seating plan as students will often gravitate toward their friends for a good chat when the regular teacher is away.

© 1996 by The Center for Applied Research in Education

The Daybook Form (Figure 5–6)

The daybook form is used to outline those lessons, procedures and events that are necessary for each class each day. This form will keep you organized and task directed. Used properly, it will reflect the daily work needed for your overall unit plans.

Daybook forms should be kept in a separate binder after their day is over. You can refer back to a particular day and see what information absent students missed. These used day plans are a great help when doing work on the same units next year.

If you are interviewed by directors of education or superintendents of instruction, you can refer them to your old daybook forms to show the development and presentation of units, dates of evaluation and procedures of instruction used in the past.

The Record of Grades and Test Marks Form (Figure 5–7)

Every teacher needs a tool to record his or her results from evaluation. The record sheet provided here allows you to keep all the student's marks on one concise form. There is an area for you to mark the subject that is being evaluated as well as the date of the evaluation.

It is always good to photocopy and lock up these record sheets once they are full or completed.

(Figure 5–5)

SEATING PLAN

Grade: _____   Teacher: _____

BACK OF CLASS

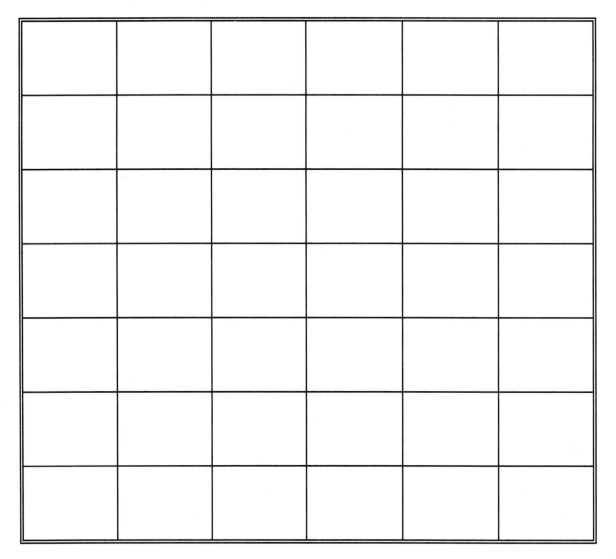

FRONT OF CLASS

NOTES:

(Figure 5–6)

DAYBOOK FORM

Day _____   Date _____

Period	Class	Lesson Data

Notes:

(Figure 5–7)

RECORD OF GRADES AND TEST MARKS

Date of Evaluation														
Subject														
Student's Name														

95. THE SUBSTITUTE'S BAG OF TRICKS

Problem: Many substitute teachers are called in to teach a class where there has been little, if anything, prepared due to extenuating circumstances, or a substitute may be called in to supervise a class where he or she has no expertise (e.g., chemistry) and the regular teacher is reluctant to have someone else in the environment (lab).

In other situations, the regular teacher will say in the preparation notes that he or she wants you to change an idea or approach to suit the circumstance of the class.

Sometimes when the regular teacher's assignment is completed early, the substitute teacher will have a blank space of time to fill until the end of the period.

How can a substitute teacher be prepared for the unexpected circumstances and special occasions when he or she needs more than the materials provided by the regular teacher?

Solution: A substitute teacher should prepare his or her own bag of goodies or data package that is made up of universally applicable materials. This package could include word search puzzles, math puzzles, crossword puzzles, word games, math sheets, a universal spelling assignment, a prioritizing assignment and so forth. The substitute's bag of goodies should include instructions on how to play many of the Spelling Bee or word quiz games that are available today. A good box of age-appropriate trivia game questions would be a positive addition to the substitute's bag of goodies or ideas.

The materials should be photocopied by the substitute, so he or she does not have to rely on the hiring school's photocopy systems. When a substitute is well prepared with enjoyable educational ideas that apply universally to students, it gives the substitute a better handle on the class which does not know him or her. Greater behavior control is attained and more efficient learning of information is achieved.

96. THE COLORFUL GENERIC LESSON PLAN FILE

Problem: Some teachers will come to school feeling ill or even downright sick because it is a problem preparing a lesson plan for a substitute teacher.

Many times the subject material cannot be taught by the substitute (e.g., calculus) and therefore, a whole new set of lesson plans must be developed to accommodate the substitute. In this situation, many teachers, while not feeling well, will say, "I might just as well go to work because it is less of a hassle or just as much of a problem to make a new lesson plan as it is to go to class."

How can a teacher always be prepared for a substitute?

Solution: Create a set of generic or universal lesson plans in your subject area that can be pulled out of your files by the substitute teacher.

This set of lesson plans would normally be for a full day's work and could include periodically updated review materials for your subject. The data in the plans should be self-motivating or require little or no direction from the substitute, thus freeing him or her from needing specific knowledge in your subject area.

It is best to place these lesson plans in a brightly colored file folder. This will make identification of the plans much easier for the substitute. The school secretary would just tell the substitute to go to your file drawer and pull out the red file and "presto," the substitute is in business.

The set of generic lesson plans is great when you are really sick. You know you have no preparation to do. It makes for peace of mind.

© 1996 by The Center for Applied Research in Education

97. AWARDS NIGHT NOMINATION FORM

Problem: Many schools have awards night at the end of the school year or term. The teachers usually get together a few weeks ahead of time to decide which students get the honors.

This is not so simple as it sounds. Many times more than one teacher will teach the same subject area but have differing grading systems, and those teachers, by nature, tend to stress different areas of the curriculum.

The awards-granting procedure must be seen by all to be objective and as equitable as possible. How do you achieve this state of objective bliss?

Solution: As part of the awards information gathering, use the Awards-Night Nomination Form (Figure 5–8). This form consists of ten social criteria that will help you decide who should get the accolades.

These criteria allow for the scoring of the teachers' opinions on a scale of four to ten for each area. This is important because the test marks do not "show it all." It is true that the social interaction of the students in the classroom is of value when making an awards decision.

Ideally, the scores on this nomination form should be combined with the grade scores to give a more complete picture of who should be honored.

(Figure 5–8)

AWARDS NIGHT
Nomination Form

_____

Award

_____   _____

Name of Student   **Name of Teacher**

	Low		Average			High	
	4	5	6	7	8	9	10
Need							
Dependability							
Leadership							
Courtesy							
Maturity							
Attitude Toward School & Course							
Citizenship							
Temperament							
Ability to Get Along With Others							
Accomplishment							

Total   _____

Average   _____

Grand
Total   _____

98. MYTHS OF THE TEACHING PROFESSION

Problem: There are certain myths of teaching that seem to have developed within and without the profession. These myths can lead to stereotyping and behavior expectations.

How can you be made aware of the myths of the teaching profession, so you can deal with them when they crop up?

Solution: Read the following list of myths that relate to your occupation.

1. Teaching is a 9:00 A.M. to 3:30 P.M. profession with an hour off for lunch.
2. If you ignore improper behavior, it will go away.
3. To make a child behave, you must make her or him feel bad.
4. When administrators hire a teacher, they are only concerned about credentials; classroom control is secondary.
5. When Betty or Johnny goes to school, the teachers will straighten her or him out.
6. Judging from the skills of this student, the teacher/school/programs he or she had last year were inadequate.
7. When we went to school and got into trouble, we received twice as much trouble at home.
8. Kids don't need dignity; they need direction.
9. You do not need to reinforce positive behavior.
10. Students have to like their teachers before they can learn from them.
11. The city is where the real problem students are.
12. When we went to school, the strap (corporal punishment) sure straightened us out.
13. Teachers just don't care anymore.
14. Students just don't care anymore.
15. Students can't tell if you are unprepared or don't know the material.
16. Once a student is a behavior problem, he or she is always a behavior problem.
17. If a student's background is abominable, the child will be abominable.
18. Men do not make good early childhood education teachers.
19. The Three R's are the only important part of education.
20. If budgets are cut, teachers can make do with less.
21. The pupil-teacher ratio is a teacher problem.
22. The best bang for the buck is to put money into post-secondary education.
23. Teachers are overpaid.

99. GUARDIAN ANGEL WEEK/MONTH

Problem: There are times during the school year when it would be just great to have a series of perks for everyone on staff.

How can the staff positively reinforce one another?

Solution: Develop the secret Guardian Angel perk-giving idea.

This idea requires the cooperation of staff members and administration.

All the teachers' names are placed in a draw box, and each teacher picks a name of another staff member from the box. Once everyone has drawn a name, they are to keep it secret. For the next week or month, the staff is to buy or make perks for one another. Ideally, the perk should be placed in the recipient's mailbox or placed on a staffroom table with the receiver's name on it. Under no circumstances is the giver to reveal his or her name.

A regular schedule of gift giving should be decided upon ahead of time, so that no one remains "perkless" for an extended period. The amount of money spent on a gift should be limited. No-cost perk-giving times really bring out the creativity in teachers.

The secret Guardian Angel perk-giving idea can do wonders for teachers, as gift receivers arrive at class trying to figure out who sent them a dozen petunias.

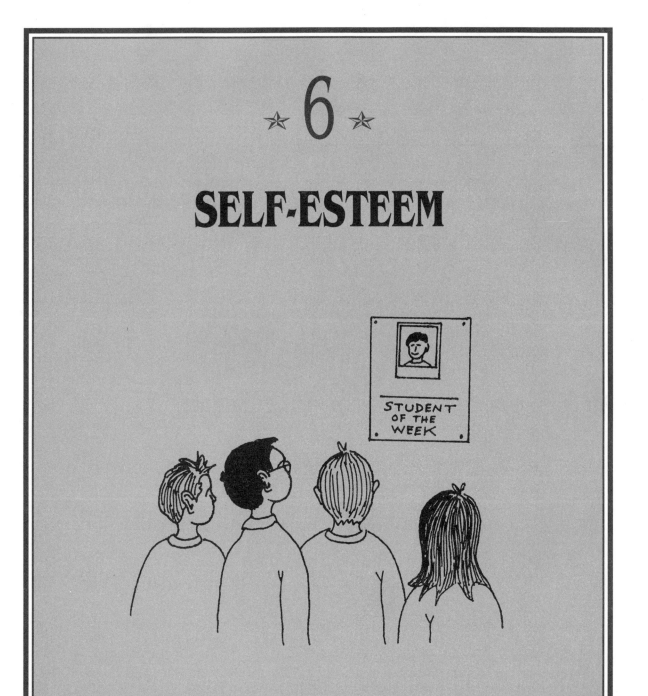

✫ 6 ✫

SELF-ESTEEM

Every student needs the intangible good feeling that comes from knowing he or she is a person of worth.

It makes great sense to teachers. If a student doesn't have any negative baggage and feels good about her- or himself, that student is easier to teach.

These self-esteem concepts are of value for a variety of students and require no highly detailed processes or lengthy time frames in order to implement.

Students need to know you care. The ideas in our Self-Esteem section prove just that.

100. THE BUMPER STICKER P.R. TOOL

Problem: You want to build the self-esteem of your students and their parents. In the process, you would like to enhance positive public relations in the community for your school. How do you accomplish this threefold task with just one idea?

Solution: Create bumper stickers for parents to put on their cars. These bumper stickers will advertise a student's status and thereby strengthen the good feelings for your school in the community. For example, if a student attains honor role standing during a particular term, the parents of the child would be given a bumper sticker that reads, "Our Daughter Is On the Honor Roll at Wilson High School." Many parents would be thrilled to place this type of bumper sticker on their vehicle.

With this idea, the esteem of the student is built up, the parents feel great, and the community at large is made aware of the positive nature of your school.

101. "STUDENT OF THE WEEK" AND SELF-ESTEEM

Problem: Many students who come through our classroom doors lack a sense of self-worth. There are precious few people in this world who give them positive reinforcement. How can we tell a child he or she is a person of worth? How do you promote self-esteem in a specific student in a dramatic way?

Solution: Choose a student every week (or two) from a draw box (allows for random selection) and do a positive write-up on that child. You may not want to use a draw box if you desire to target specific students. These may be students who would sincerely benefit from some recognition.

The write-up and/or the student's picture is then exhibited on a colorful poster in a prominent spot in the hallway.

A trophy may be given to that student for the week as well as a certificate indicating that this student is being honored.

A logical extension of the "Student of the Week" concept is to display the pictures of several students who are excelling in a specific area, such as math. You will find it of value to focus on students who are the top grade point average or who have shown the most improvement from one term or test to another.

The idea here is to exhibit the student's picture with a short positive write-up about his or her performance. This can only serve to make the student feel good. These ideas not only lead to growth in the self-esteem of the student, it also creates a feeling of warm fuzzies for the school by the students and parents alike.

© 1996 by The Center for Applied Research in Education

Best Suited for
Special Students at Any Grade Level

102. THE SPECIAL STUDENT REPORT FORM

Problem: Many special needs students are now being placed in the regular class-room. For various reasons, parents of these special needs children see this as an opportunity to "normalize" their children into the school system.

This is a great idea in many respects; however, when it comes to reporting to the parents as to the performance of a special needs child, what frame of reference do you use? You cannot compare that child with the mainstream. If you do, he or she will fail miserably, thus compounding the problem with this child and his or her parents.

How do you give a fair assessment of the special needs student that is not based on some objective evaluation, such as a test?

Solution: Use the anecdotal-based reporting tool called The Special Student Report Form (Figure 6–1).

This form allows the teacher to give a comprehensive report to the parents on how well the special needs student is functioning in the school environment.

The student is compared with himself or herself. Important changes in behavior can be seen as these reports are compared over the school year. This is of far greater value to the parents of the special needs child than grade scores.

The six concepts of independence, dependability, personal initiative, honesty, relating to others and personal appearance are important for personal growth and development for eventual independent living.

Each of these concepts is broken down further to include actual day-to-day working components. These components are the behaviors the teacher sees every day. In the normal bump and grind of events, the teacher is called upon to be aware of these components and mark them on a reporting form at any time.

The Special Student Report Form can be sent to the parents at any time during the school year. It would be of particular benefit to the parents of the special needs student if the report form went home more frequently than three or four times a year, as the regular report cards do.

(Figure 6–1)

NAME: _____   DATE: _____

THE SPECIAL STUDENT REPORT FORM

CONCEPTS	COMPONENTS	EXCELLENT	GOOD	POOR
INDEPENDENCE	Begins work without being told			
	Does not need continuous reassurance			
	Does not excessively ask for help			
DEPENDABILITY	Student is punctual			
	Attends school regularly			
	Completes task			
	Follows directions			
PERSONAL INITIATIVE	Begins work when assigned			
	Does not sit idle—seeks teacher's help			
	Adapts to different situations			
HONESTY	Seeks permission			
	Tells the truth			
	No theft behavior			
RELATING TO OTHERS	Good communication and cooperation with teachers			
	No eruptions of anger			
	Has good manners and is polite			
	Does not complain excessively			
	Handles constructive criticism properly			
PERSONAL APPEARANCE	Student is clean with neatly combed hair			
	Student dresses appropriately			

103. CLEVER KID QUALITY QUESTIONS

Problem: Your math class is like a mosaic society in terms of the range of skills. Some are very low, most are in the middle, but a few would give Einstein a run for his money.

How do you challenge those brighter kids who are performing at a higher level on a daily basis? How do you prevent the budding thermal physicist in your class from becoming bored?

Solution: Use Clever Kid Quality Questions. When you assign your normal amount of math work from your regular math text, also assign Clever Kid Quality Questions from other resources. Tell the students they do not have to do them; they are only for enrichment. They are only for those students who think they have the skills to do them.

The results will amaze you. The advanced math students will gladly gobble up the new questions and so will some of the middle-of-the road students. Those who are struggling with the regular assignment usually won't venture a try, but they will work harder on what they are doing.

Now before you say, "This is just adding extra work onto the good students," you are right, but you must be creative as to where you get those extra questions for the bright students to do. The best idea is to get a defunct or out-of-use textbook from one grade above where your students are and take the questions from there. It is not a good idea to take questions from a current text one year above you because the teacher next year has to take those same students through that program when he or she gets them. You could be faced with an angry colleague.

Brighter students love to think they can do work that is above their grade level. This, in itself, is incentive enough for the sharp mathematical intellect.

104. THE PROGRESS ROLL

Problem: Many students are hard working yet they never seem to make the honor roll. Many lower ability yet very diligent students get little if any recognition in a formal way. How do we recognize the success of all the hard workers and not just the high achieving honor roll students?

Solution: In order to reinforce the success of the top students as well as the hard working mid-achievers, you should develop a progress roll as a replacement for the honor roll or as a supplement to it.

The criteria for being named to the progress roll would normally include those items used for the honor roll plus whatever reasons you would want to use to include a hard working mid-achiever. You may decide to have only academic improvement as your yardstick or you may decide to expand your standards to include social or sports participation reasons.

105. THE POSTCARD P.R. IDEA

Problem: You need a positive and powerful public relations tool that facilitates open and effective communication between the teachers and the parents of the children attending your school.

Solution: Send the parents and child a positive postcard (Figure 6–2). The postcard will inform the parents of their son's or daughter's excellent performance. This direct note from the teacher will normally only speak of the admirable aspects of the child's behavior. You can tell the parents their child is intellectually strong in certain areas of school work or you may want to expand the postcard to include any part of school life.

The postcard is a concrete helpful tool that goes beyond mere verbalization. It will brighten the day of any parent receiving it and it will often be shown to friends and relatives of the child. This will reinforce the observed good behavior as well as help to develop goodwill between the school and the parents.

The postcard itself can be one of those purchased at the local drug store or you may want to be ambitious and have a few hundred made at a print shop with your school logo emblazoned on the front. Whichever you choose, you will find that the Postcard P.R. system will be one of the warmest of fuzzies you can ever send to parents. The overall results will touch many a heart.

(Figure 6–2)

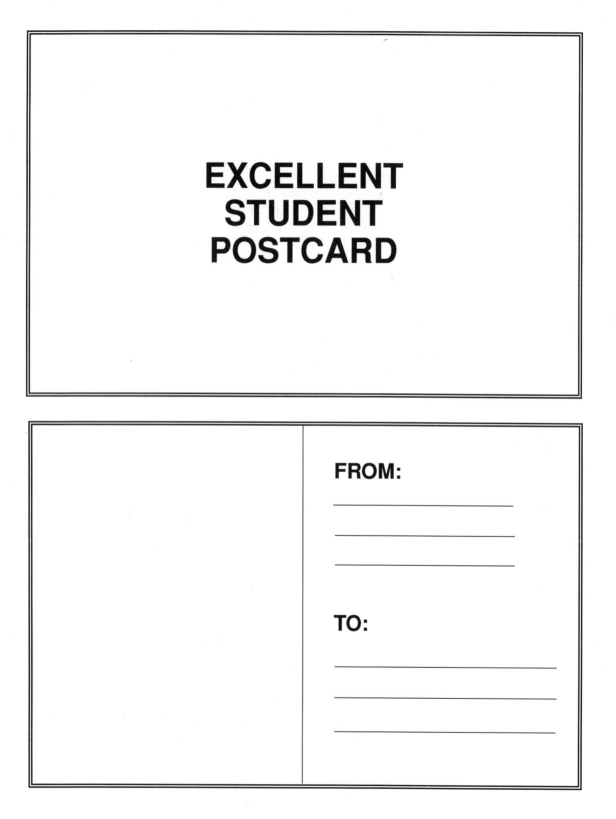

EXCELLENT STUDENT POSTCARD

FROM:

TO:

106. CHILDREN OF WORTH

Problem: Many of our students lack self-esteem. We know that many young, impressionable people have had a hard time of it in life and it shows. Many students never receive a hug from a parent or anyone just to tell them they have done well. A large number of students need to know they are people of worth.

What can you do to help break down that established barrier of negative self-worth?

Solution: Target a student you feel needs an uplift. Identify one aspect of that child that is good or unique. In this human dynamic you will see that everyone has something of worth about them physically or socio/emotionally.

Give that student an award (Figure 6–3) for his or her particular uniqueness even if it means giving a child recognition for having the best dimples of any other student in the class.

I have seen this work quite dramatically. Many students will latch on to this recognition. It becomes a valued and therefore important circumstance in his or her life. The self-esteem is strongly bolstered in the child as he or she interacts with the other students.

To reinforce this idea, you may wish to display the picture of the student on the wall or simply list the award winners and their attributes in a prominent location in the classroom.

To further develop this idea you could enlist one or two of the parents of the students to bake a small cake that would be shared when you honor the student with the best "dimples!"

(Figure 6–3)

This Is To Certify

_____

is a

Student of Worth

* Outstanding behavior

* Special skills

* A positive person to have in the class

107. THE EXCELLENT STUDENT RECOGNITION AWARD

Problem: How do you reward those good students who are consistent in their performance, courteous and a genuine joy to have in the classroom?

How do we positively reinforce the sometimes-neglected students at or near the top of the academic ladder?

Solution: Give this quiet, independent, hard-working, pleasant student the Excellent Student Recognition Award. This award is unique in that it gives double reinforcement to the child.

The award is initially given to the student as he or she is called to the principal's office. The student is told about the things that he or she consistently does that are an asset to him or her and to the school. The principal then phones the parents while the student is in the office. The principal tells the parents of the excellent performance and behavior of their child and then sends the Excellent Student Recognition Award (Figure 6–4) letter home to the parents of the student.

The letter we include here is a sample of what the award letter should look like. It is best if this letter is retyped using the information that pertains to your school and to the student you are recognizing.

(Figure 6–4)

SAMPLE LETTER

November 28

Dear Mr. & Mrs. Bartel and Kathy:

Too often in a job like mine, we spend about 90% of our time with our "problem" students, and the efforts and achievements of our good students—while recognized—seem to go unmentioned. In an effort to remedy this situation somewhat, I decided to write to all the Grade 8 students and their parents/guardians if the student achieved an average of 80% or higher at the November reporting period.

I want to tell you how pleased we are at Wilson High School with Kathy's academic performance so far this year, and also that I am pleased to place Kathy on the **TERM ONE HONOR ROLL. With an average of 82.6%, Kathy ranks 21st out of 146 students in her grade**. Kathy seems to have adjusted to the new school quite well. Her attitude, achievement, and behavior are good, and we are pleased to have Kathy as a student. We are looking forward to a continued good effort.

Should you have any concerns, please do not hesitate to call us at the school or drop in for a visit.

Sincerely yours,

Principal

108. THE ETHNIC DIVERSITY CANDLE

Problem: You want to stress the importance of the ethnic diversity of your classroom. One look at the students in front of you, and you can see the epitome of the expression "melting pot society." You want to show that in your society, the cultures become inter-twined and operate together for the good of all.

How can you graphically display to the children the importance of the mixing, acceptance and working together with people of different ethnic backgrounds?

Solution: Make the Ethnic Diversity Candle. You will need some basic candle making skills and a candle mold for this idea.

Initially, you need to identify the various ethnic backgrounds that exist in your classroom. Once the children have a knowledge of what their roots are, you then gather the students into ethnic groups. You then give each student in each ethnic group a large colored wax crayon. There is to be only one color for each ethnic group. For example, the students with Scottish backgrounds might all have brown crayons and all the students in the French group might have purple crayons.

The color distribution of crayons to the ethnic groups is at the discretion of the teacher. You should be sensitive to any ethnic group that would traditionally like or not like a certain color.

The next step is to melt the crayons in a pot. (This would be a good time to explain what the term "melting pot society" means.) The teacher would facilitate this by calling up each ethnic group one at a time and have them place their crayons into the pot to be melted. Once all the crayons have entered the pot, the teacher is to stir the melting crayons just enough so that the colors of the crayons are still distinct, yet are seen to be interweaved with each other.

Once the teacher feels there is a good mixture and the wick is in place, it is time to pour the liquified crayons into the candle mold. When the wax has cooled, the candle is to be removed from the mold in front of the bright onlooking eyes of the students.

The finished candle will graphically display the intermixing of the colors from each ethnic group. Each color is necessary to help make the complete candle as each ethnic group is necessary to help make our society complete.

© 1996 by The Center for Applied Research in Education

109. PICTURE THIS

Problem: You want to feature your students in some form of display in the school. You would like that display to be in a totally natural setting.

How can you show parents and visitors that your school is a student-centered environment?

Solution: Become the roving photographer for your school. Your main goal is to photograph students in as natural a pose and setting as possible.

The resultant pictures should be displayed on a bulletin board or in a trophy case that is at the height of the students. If you photograph the students fairly often and keep renewing the display, you will end up with a collection of excellent shots. In this way you will be able to feature every student at least once each school year. It is at this point that you can use the old pictures for an increased P.R. value. The pictures that are no longer on display can be placed in the student's report card on report card day. The parents will treasure pictures of their child in the positive natural setting of your school.

⭐ 7 ⭐

TEACHER AND STUDENT PROTECTION IDEAS

In order for you and your students to focus attention completely on learning, you must have freedom from those political and circumstantial stressors that can often be the result of working with people. Any one of the partners in the education process can have overriding demands upon your time and energy. Teachers must learn to react appropriately to real and potential stress-producing situations.

Teacher and Student Protection Ideas contains just what the title suggests. In here are solid, tested concepts that safeguard you and your students from the variety of problems that detract from learning.

110. TEACHERS' STRESS-REDUCTION SURVIVAL GUIDELINES

Problem: Teachers in our society are a very well-educated group of individuals who can have a positive influence on the direction of people's lives. Those educators take their responsibility seriously and have strongly fulfilled that mandate. Almost every community leader or influential businessperson will tell you his or her success is due at least in part to a teacher who cared.

In the process of achieving their mandate, teachers must deal with people of every description, lifestyle and set of expectations. This can lead to stress.

If teachers are to have long and productive careers, they must learn to identify and work with stress and the things that cause stress to occur.

How can teachers identify stressors and consciously work to overcome pressures in their work environment?

Solution: The following is a set of guidelines designed to be effective in helping you cope with the stressors of your profession.

1. Take a good look at your staffroom. If you find yourself carrying extra or negative baggage out of there, stay away from the staffroom.

2. Identify overly critical or protective parents. Dot your i's and cross your t's when dealing with their child. Keep a file.

3. Learn to listen to your colleagues but remember that the person you work with may only want to verbally dump his or her problem and not necessarily want you to take action. It is his or her situation, not yours. You don't borrow someone else's problem. You purchase it.

4. Recognize times when it is best to keep your mouth shut.

5. Don't sweat the small stuff. If a parent wants you to get rid of the geraniums because he or she thinks the child is allergic to them—get rid of the geraniums.

6. Put more laughter into your life. Have a clean joke time. Every student must come with and be able to tell a clean, nondemeaning joke. Have students write down their favorites to tell their parents.

7. Whistle or hum as you work during preparation times. "Music soothes the soul of the savage beast."

8. Walk to school, join a health or exercise club. You have heard many times that walking is the best exercise. A walk of at least two miles per day will do wonders for your sense of well being.

9. Do not participate in the bad mouthing of another teacher or administrator. This is not ethical. You will worry that what you said will get back to that person.

10. Get a hobby.

11. Keep a spare set of school keys handy in case yours get lost.

12. Use the professional counseling resources available to you should you feel it is necessary. Don't be an island unto yourself. Believe it or not, you are only human.

13. Listen to the advice of more experienced and respected teachers.

14. Wear comfortable clothing. Support and promote blue jean days and dress-down days for the staff.

15. Eat properly. Read the label on that bag of potato chips before you think of eating them.

16. Don't watch the late news before you go to bed. The problems of the world do have an effect on your conscious and subconscious psychic space.

17. Do a crossword puzzle in bed before you go to sleep. The world does not really appreciate the medicinal effects of a crossword puzzle. It causes you to focus your mind on nonthreatening, noncrisis, yet challenging thoughts.

18. Do not associate with people who are always unhappy or bitter. It seems every staff has one of these.

19. Remember, if you are having trouble with a difficult student, so is everyone else.

20. Keep a fairly big cookie in your desk.

21. Create something for yourself to look forward to, i.e., a college class, a holiday, a visit to a friend.

22. Forgive those who trespass against you. If you don't, the bitterness you hold for some other person will turn inward and hurt you. You see, the person you are bitter toward usually doesn't care.

23. Try to actually believe that it's "o.k." for you to make a mistake even if you are achievement oriented.

24. Make a positive contribution to your society. Join a service club, church or community organization. It will give you a sense of worth to help others outside the confines of your employment.

25. Don't drink too much coffee or other caffeine-heavy beverages.

26. Try to schedule some time alone for yourself each day.

27. If your circumstances will allow, buy a dog or cat. It will love you unconditionally.

28. Remember, at the end of a day, a bathtub is worth more than the Crown Jewels.

111. LATE ASSIGNMENT INFORMATION SHEET

Problem: There are some students who will either refuse to hand in an assignment or will be extremely tardy in doing so. This can cause problems if you were going to use the grade from that assignment as part of your term mark. In the real world of today's classroom, you, the teacher, are often found at fault if there is no grade or missing grades for a particular student's term mark. How can you protect yourself by showing you have fulfilled your responsibility in relation to these students and that the complete responsibility for the missed or late assignment is upon the student's shoulders?

Solution: When a student does not complete an assignment or point blank refuses to cooperate and even start the work, have the student sign a late assignment information sheet (Figure 7–1) that you have filled in. You tell the student that you need this paper signed for your records because there is no assignment and this paper takes its place until the assignment is completed and handed in to you.

The late assignment information sheet simply indicates that you had fulfilled your responsibility toward the student.

The sheet confirms the fact that:

a)   You assigned the work.

b)   You asked for the work a number of times.

c)   Students had access to the materials to do the work.

d)   The student did not do the work.

e)   The student signed the paper agreeing with this data.

The Late Assignment Information Sheet does not say the work will never be done. It simply states the facts as they are.

The stress-saving aspect of this is the fact that if the student never does do the work and the resultant grade is low, you have a form to show the parents indicating that the fault in not completing the work lies solely with their child.

© 1996 by The Center for Applied Research in Education

(Figure 7–1)

LATE ASSIGNMENT INFORMATION SHEET

DATE:_____   DATE DUE:_____

I, _____ , have been

asked _____ times to hand in my _____

ASSIGNMENT. To date, I have not handed this work to the teacher.

I have received the necessary information to produce this work.

Student Signature: _____

Teacher Signature: _____

112. THE PROTECTIVE VOLUNTEER IDEA

Problem: There are times during the school year when you must remove a specific person(s) from an ongoing class without the rest of the students knowing or suspecting something is "up" or that you are on to something.

The problem is especially acute when the class knows Mary or John to be in some kind of trouble. Some students are quite sensitive and would be extremely embarrassed if you entered a classroom and asked them to leave or go to the principal's office. Some students are not so kind as others. When this type of child sees one of his or her peers being called out of the class, you may end up with a student being laughed at or even ridiculed, thus compounding the problem.

Solution: When it is necessary to get a student out of the class in a hurry without anyone suspecting something is amiss, ask for a volunteer. Tell the students you need help with a situation. You desire a person to help you right now. You stress the urgent nature of the problem so as not to give them a chance to put two and two together and figure out what you are doing.

Immediately most hands will go up to volunteer because to volunteer usually means you get out of the classroom to do some task. Once the hands have gone up in eager anticipation, you then choose the student you intended to take out in the first place.

With a good introduction, you should be able to get every hand raised on the first try. You have to make the thing they are volunteering for seen as a thing of worth. This increases your chances of getting the one you want to put his or her hand up.

But what if the student you want does not put up his or her hand and almost everyone else does? You simply say this to the students, "There are too many of you to choose from. I can't be fair so I think I'll take the person who doesn't have his/her hand up." You then take the student you wanted in the first place.

The beauty of this technique is basically twofold; either you got the person you wanted out of the classroom or you protected the student from false accusations if the person you removed from the class was not the right one. If indeed you do have the right student the first time, then you can discuss your problems with this student as soon as you get away from prying eyes. If, however, you singled out the wrong student, then after the necessary investigation you can return that student to the class with no harm done. You have protected your wrong choice from false accusations.

This volunteer system has an extra little feature. You are also not showing the rest of the class that you have knowledge about that "fight" in the school yard or about the "stolen" property or whatever the case may be. You not only protect the student's right to privacy, you protect your own rights in this area.

This technique is unusual in that it seems to work over and over with the same class. I have used it more than once in the same day and no one caught on that I was simply selecting students out in order to have them answer a series of questions about a school problem.

113. THE INCOMPLETE MATH TECHNIQUE

Problem: You have a large class of junior high school students. In this class are a number of nonaggressive types who will not do their homework or other assigned tasks. You perceive that these students have parents who are critical of the teacher at every turn. The students are failing math and you, the teacher, are being blamed.

Solution: Write **INCOMPLETE** in bold letters after each assignment that is not done. This technique is designed to show the student and the parents that the work assigned is not finished and that you did indeed assign the work and that the student failed to uphold his or her end of the arrangement.

What happens here is that a series of incompletes begins to show up in the negligent student's notebook. When you face the parents you take the notebook and show them the number of incompletes written in it. This focuses the responsibility for the work on the student.

This idea makes the student aware of his or her responsibilities. The bold incompletes are hard to ignore and will soon become a thing to be avoided by doing the required work.

114. PLACEBO NOTE IDEA

Problem: Some students in your school have head lice. The problem lies with a certain student or group of students. You need to send a note home to the parents of those students in order to tell them what procedures to follow. You know some students in your class who suspect something is "up" will make fun of those who get the letter.

How can you protect the students in question from ridicule?

Solution: Give all the students in your class a sealed letter or note at the end of the day. The idea is to give the students whom you have identified as having the problem a different note from the students who do not have the lice.

The parents of the students with lice or scabies (the itch mite) should be called and the problem discussed. The parents of the students who do not have the problem should be told to keep a watch for any signs of lice occurring on their child.

The fact that you give everyone a note will allow those with the problem to have some anonymity and, therefore, not be mocked or made fun of by some of the less caring children.

115. TEST SECURITY SYSTEMS

Problem: You are teaching more than one class in a particular subject, grade 9 math, for example. You are using the same materials for instruction for each class. As a natural extension of this, you plan to use the same evaluation tool or test for each of those classes.

Assuming you can't put the test on the blackboard but rather have a preprinted test form as most of us do, you will need some type of security system to insure that a copy of your evaluation device does not circulate to the other classes you teach.

Solution: There are three possible solutions:

a) Staple the answer sheets to the question paper wherein both must be handed in together.

b) Have students answer the questions right on the question sheet.

c) Have the students write their names on the question sheet as well as the answer sheet. Both the answer sheet and the question sheet are then handed in together. With the names of the students on the test question paper you can easily check to see if one is missing and which student did not hand in the question paper. This system will prevent a copy of your test question sheet from circulating to student friends in other classes to whom you teach the same subject.

116. BEHAVIOR RECORD SHEET

Problem: In the classroom you will encounter many behavior problems. This unfortunately is a "given" with the job nowadays. Society has become more liberal and values as well as goals and directions are vague at best for many people. As a direct function of this situation you, the teacher, will not be seen as "right" in many situations involving students. I don't need to tell you that often times when you discipline a child, the parents of that child will not agree that you have justification for your actions and indeed will blame you for the totality of the problem. (Welcome to the club.)

You must therefore protect yourself if you are to be an effective teacher in today's environment. The blanket respect for the teacher that somewhat existed years ago certainly does not exist today.

Solution: If you recognize a particular student as a potential behavior problem or recognize that certain parents are highly critical, then you should keep an anecdotal file on that student. Keep a consistent record of that child's in-school behavior with witnesses to back up your position. I include a tool for this purpose. This is the Behavior Record Sheet (Figure 7–2). With this, you can list the student's behaviors in a consistent professional manner which is far better than a jumble of paper slips chucked into a file.

The reason for the Behavior Record Sheet will become obvious when you find it necessary to have contact with parents. If you have a student "up on the carpet" for a particular behavior, the parents will inevitably ask you this question: "Has my child ever done anything like this before?" If you do not have written evidence of his or her poor behaviors readily available supporting the problems you now have with the student, the parents quite often will shrug off this event as a one-time occurrence. You may be left with the problem not solved and lacking credibility in the circumstance.

A body of evidence with the names of witnesses will add a great deal of strength to your persistence in this matter. Your main aim of improved behavior for the ultimate good of the student is more likely to receive action if you are well prepared.

(Figure 7–2)

BEHAVIOR RECORD SHEET

STUDENT NAME: _____

DATE: _____

TIME: _____   CLASS: _____

TEACHER: _____

OBSERVED BEHAVIORS: _____

_____

_____

_____

_____

_____

_____

WITNESS(ES): _____

****

ACTION TAKEN: _____

_____

_____

_____

PARENT CONTACT (IF ANY) BY: _____

_____

TEACHER: _____

117. GUIDELINES FOR AVOIDANCE OF FALSE ACCUSATIONS OF SEXUAL OR PHYSICAL ABUSE

Problem: More and more teachers are being falsely accused of sexual or physical abuse of their students.

You have all read the headlines. I do not need to overstate it. This is a worry for many of us in our profession. Up until recently most of the accusations have been directed at male teachers; however, an ever increasing number of female teachers are now being falsely accused of this form of deviance.

I have searched personally and through my teachers' organization for an insurance package that would protect us from the false accusations we encounter. Of the large number of insurance companies queried, not one had a package that would give us some protection in this area.

Solution: Our only protection at this point is the adherence to the following set of guidelines.

1. Teach with the classroom door open. If the door must be closed, then insist that there be a window installed in the door. This will show the courts that there was no intention on your part to entrap the students.

2. Do not be alone in a classroom (or other room) with a single student. Counseling should be done in an open area such as a library or common area.

3. When you have to discipline a student, do so in front of a colleague witness.

4. When on field trips take an adult of the opposite gender with you.

5. Do not sit beside a student on a bus or van.

6. Never transport a single student in a vehicle. Take others as witnesses.

7. Do not touch any student.

8. Do not let any student touch you.

9. Be careful when checking the dressing/shower rooms of your (volleyball) team. Unless you can't avoid it, do not enter until all students have departed.

118. STUDENT SIGNAL CHART

Problem: Some students come to school with social-emotional baggage. Many students are from unstable or weak family backgrounds that cause them to enter the school doors angry or upset over some situation or event. Your normal student can have that "bad day." These students can cause trouble, to say the least. He or she can explode with little or no provocation, leaving you wondering what the cause was. How can you head off trouble with this type of student? How can you be made aware of the student's state of mind, so you can help him or her through the day?

Solution: Use the Student Signal Chart (Figure 7–3). This chart is designed to signal the teacher as to where a particular student is at emotionally. It can be used either individually or with a group of students sitting at a table.

The Student Signal Chart has three basic components. The first is a scale of one to ten. The students are told to circle a number on the chart as to how they feel. To circle a ten would tell you the student is having a great day with a lot of positive things happening to him or her. To circle a one or a two would signal to the teacher that this day is not good for him or her and indeed is bordering on rotten. This is often the most crucial information for you to have in terms of conflict avoidance with that student.

The second part of the Student Signal Chart tells you whether or not the student wishes to talk about his or her problem.

In the third part of the chart, you will see a few lines where the student can express how he or she feels about the circumstances. Sometimes students will not talk about their problems, but they will write them down for you. The space provided for this purpose allows the student to mentally dump his or her feelings on paper. This in itself will have a calming effect on the student.

The setting wherein you collect this emotional data can vary. You may want to have a group meeting each morning where all students fill in the Signal Chart, or you may ask the students to use them as they feel it is necessary, any time during the school day.

The Student Signal Chart opens communication to you, the teacher, at a time when the student is emotionally distraught and possibly needing help. Positive interactions among the students are promoted when a student signals a high score on the chart. The student should then be encouraged to tell others of his or her good news or good fortune. It makes a good sharing time for all.

© 1996 by The Center for Applied Research in Education

(Figure 7–3)

STUDENT SIGNAL CHART

This is how I feel today   10   just wonderful

(circle appropriate number)   9

                                     8

                                     7

                                     6

                                     5   a normal/average day

                                     4

                                     3

                                     2

                                     1   down in the dumps

Yes, I do want to talk to the teacher about how I feel.

No, I do not want to talk to the teacher about how I feel.

- -

This is why I feel the way I do _____

_____

_____

_____

_____

                                   _____

                                          Student's Name

119. GIBRALTAR PASSWORD

Problem: Many parents on occasion are unable to get to the school on time to pick their children up as they would normally do. Those parents will often send a friend or neighbor to the school to pick up their children and drive them home.

In today's culture the very real problems of child abuse, kidnapping and custody battles are not far from us. How does a child or teacher know whether the person coming to pick up a student has indeed been sent by the parent(s) or guardian of that child?

Solution: You, as the teacher, should work with the school office to establish a password system between students and their parents or guardians. Each family should establish a password that is secret to that family. It is not to be shared with others.

Students are to be instructed to ask the person who is supposed to be giving him or her a ride for the password. If the person in the vehicle does not know the password, the student is not to go with him or her. The password itself should be a word that would not usually come up as part of a normal conversation. A word such as "Gibraltar" is a good example.

Once you establish the password system, you need to keep a record of each student's password for your own verification purposes.

You may find it necessary to have a field trip password. In the event a student should get separated from your group, it would be very important for a student to have the protection of a password if and when he or she is approached by strangers. It has occurred when some youngsters have been lost in the wilderness that they will not come out even if their name is called by a search party member because in most cases children have been repeatedly taught to not talk to strangers. The intense fright of being alone and lost in the bush sometimes only serves to heighten a child's fear of a stranger's voice. However, if he or she has been coached ahead of time to respond to a password, even if the password is spoken by a stranger, this will help alleviate the problem.

**Best Suited for
Grade 4 to High School**

120. THE EASY BACK-UP NOTE SYSTEM

Problem: You have given X amount of notes on the board in your subject area. Most of these notes were from the hard data; however, many were ad lib examples from your personal experience.

Betty and Johnny have just come up to you to say they "lost" their notes or their notes have been "stolen." They now have nothing to study from for the upcoming test.

How do you keep a spare set of quality notes that includes your personal examples and improvised details?

Solution: In a class that tends to have a high degree of note taking, such as History or French, it is a good idea to borrow a notebook every few weeks from one of the better students who has excellent handwriting and ask permission to copy and distribute those notes. When you are faced with the lost or stolen notes problem, you hand those students a copy of the good student's notes.

This idea eliminates excuses and keeps all students up to date with a current set of notes from which to study.

It is quite amazing how this technique in itself will cut down on the number of lost or stolen notebooks.

Care should be taken to make sure this idea does not encourage students to stop taking notes. It is in place only to solve the lost or stolen note problem.

121. REFUSAL PROTECTION

Problem: On occasion when you give out a test, a student may refuse or ask to be excused from writing it.

A student with very valid reasons may not have the situation suitable at home or otherwise to allow him or her to write a test on the day you pick.

At other times, a student may be just plain belligerent and, for no observable reason, will refuse to write your test.

How do you protect yourself when some parents do not understand the dynamics of their child in the classroom and want a concrete reason why their child's mark is low? How do you focus the responsibility for not writing a test onto the student where it belongs? How can you gain some insights into the nature of the student's problem in this area?

Solution: When a student does not write your assigned test or quiz, have the student tell you why. This is accomplished by filling out the Test Substitute Form (Figure 7–4). This form protects you by virtue of the fact that if the student never does write the test, then you place the completed form in the student's file ready to be extracted when you are called upon to explain why a child's mark or grade is substandard.

The name Test Substitute Form was designed to make this document as non-threatening as possible. Many times when this form is given to the student, he or she is in a heightened emotional state and to have a title such as Low Grade Reason Form would be inappropriate.

When you present the Test Substitute Form to the student, you tell that person you need some documentation to fill the place where the test mark would normally be. This form will also keep the student occupied while others are writing the test, thus cutting down on the in-class disturbances.

It is best to encourage the student to be as open as possible and not hold anything back. The form will sometimes reveal deeply set problems and, thereby, give you a better understanding of where the student is coming from. It may give you a genuine chance to get help for the student with his or her problems should that become necessary.

© 1996 by The Center for Applied Research in Education

(Figure 7–4)

TEST SUBSTITUTE FORM

DATE: _____   TEACHER NAME: _____

SUBJECT: _____   STUDENT NAME: _____

I am not able to write the test today for the following reasons:

_____

_____

_____

_____

_____

_____

If there were any other people involved in this decision, please indicate their names and describe their involvement.

_____

_____

_____

_____

_____

_____

_____
Student Signature

122. ANSWER NO-CHANGE GUIDELINES

Problem: Some students, when they get their tests back from you after being marked or graded, will seek out a way to change or add an answer. That student will then bring the test back to you saying you accidentally missed an answer or you marked one wrong when in fact it was correct.

This problem is especially prevalent in large diversified classes where it is hard to remember each student's test paper.

How do you prevent students from changing responses or answers on returned tests?

Solution: Follow the set of guidelines for the prevention of change of answers on tests.

1. When you are marking a test, make sure that you put an X on the wrong answer—not beside the wrong answer.

2. Any answer space on a test that has been left blank by a student should have an X placed on it as you mark the test. This prevents the student from filling in this space after he or she gets the test back.

3. Tell students the test must be written in nonerasable ink. Erasable pens or the use of pencils is not permitted.

4. If the problem is chronic in your class, photocopy the test papers after you have marked them. Word will soon get around that you are doing this and your problems will cease.

© 1996 by The Center for Applied Research in Education

123. CONFRONTATION, INCIDENT, ALTERCATION SURVIVAL GUIDELINES

Problem: Many teachers come across volatile or hazardous situations or altercations as they work in schools today. The problem could be anything from heated words to someone wielding a .45 caliber.

It is crucial in our society that teachers or anyone who works with the public learn how to handle and document an incident as well as work with witnesses to that incident or problem.

It has happened that in cases of more serious situations, teachers have been called to testify in court and, in some cases, teachers have become part of the litigation or lawsuit resulting from their involvement with the incident.

How do you handle and protect yourself during the actual incident? How do you document the incident in a professional manner that will help shield you in case of litigation? How do you get the best quality responses from people at the scene?

Solution: Follow the guidelines for dealing with an incident, documenting the problem and getting the best responses from a witness.

A. Dealing with an incident:

1. When coming upon a problem, take a moment to assess the situation. Ask yourself "Will my intervention help or hinder what is happening? Can I safely intervene?"

2. Do not chase after anyone who has an offensive weapon even if you think you can overpower him or her.

3. Speak calmly but firmly. If you know the parties involved, speak to them by name. Demand a stop to their actions.

4. Call for help. The person who responds can be a valuable witness as well as a help. Get their name, address and phone number.

5. If you are hit, have the self control to prevent your anger from becoming part of the problem.

6. Separate the combatants in two physical spaces, two separate walls, for example. Escort the people to the office one at a time. Use the helper to take the first person and you take the second person.

7. If the incident is serious enough, call for the police. The police are trained professionals in the area of diffusing an altercation.

8. If medical aid is required, do so only up to your level of competence. Be able to justify this. Call for medical assistance.

B.   Documenting an incident:

It is important that you write down the details of the incident as soon as you are free to do so. Your ability to remember details is hindered by time, discussion with others and the mind's tendency to suppress information in order to cope.

1.   Write down the time and date of the incident as well as the time and date of your documentation.

2.   List the events in chronological order.

3.   Describe the physical environment at the time of the incident.

4.   Describe the characteristics and the mood of the people involved.

5.   Record only the facts. Do not write down any hearsay, speculation or conjecture.

6.   Write or type neatly. Do not use flowery language.

7.   Do not erase or white out errors in your final copy. Just cross out mistakes and initial them.

8.   It is all right to use a quotation if you are absolutely sure of its authenticity.

9.   If it is possible, photograph or draw a diagram of the area. This is especially important if there is any damage associated with the incident.

10.   Write down all known relationships or biases such as race, color or creed that may be relevant to the situation.

C.   Working with a witness:

1.   Obtain the service of a recorder person to take notes and to witness your interview process. With this other person doing the writing, you are free to conduct the interview.

2.   Interview the witness quickly and privately. It is important to interview witnesses before they have contact with others because input from others can become part of a witness's report.

3.   Ask the person to tell the whole story in the order it happened.

4.   Ask the recorder to note the verbal and nonverbal or body language responses of the person being interviewed.

5.   Ask the witness to draw a diagram of the physical position of each person involved.

6.   It is important in any litigation to know if the information from the witness was given willingly or not. This must be specified.

7.   Ask questions that require a detailed answer. "Yes" or "no" responses do not expand the flow of data.

8.   Ask the person being interviewed if he or she has any details as to the background of the incident.

9.   When the interview with a witness is concluded, have the recorder read back the account to that person. Have the witness sign and date the account of events.

10.   Inform the principal or vice principal of your school about the details of the incident. Fill in any forms he or she might have. Give him or her a copy of your documentation of the events.

124. THE "PICKING TEAMS" SYSTEM

Problem: When students choose members for teams in gym or in the schoolyard, they tend to choose the best players first and omit, or leave until last, the students who do not possess great sports skills. This is often an ego-smashing experience for the child who is never picked or is last to be chosen.

What are some creative ways to choose teams wherein no student is made to feel embarrassed?

Solution: There are several techniques one can use to pick teams that are nondemeaning to any student. It is important to do this because it is necessary for the better players to see that everyone is a person of worth.

Here are a few guidelines for choosing teams:

1. Make the low-skills student the captain of the team.

2. Choose teams that will exist for a month or longer. This stops the problem from happening every day or so.

3. Tell the students that you, the teacher, will choose the last four or five remaining players for the teams. Then quickly assign these students, thus preventing embarrassment.

4. Line up the students according to the criteria listed below. When you have them lined up, you can count them off 1, 2, 1, 2, and so forth, or 1, 2, 3, if you are making three teams.

   Suggested line-up criteria:

   a) height from shortest to tallest
   b) age from oldest to youngest
   c) arm span from widest to smallest
   d) pulse rate from fastest to slowest
   e) length of hair
   f) size of smile
   g) length of index finger
   h) shoe size
   i) length from elbow to fingertip

   These line-up criteria are a great way to reinforce skills, such as estimating, comparing lengths and ordering. You can use these not only in physical education, but also in academic subjects where you need groups.

   This idea works especially well in multi-graded classrooms.

   The best feature of these ideas is that you have made team picking a safe experience for all students; thus, making the lower ability students' day just a little bit easier in life.

© 1996 by The Center for Applied Research in Education

125. LAST-MINUTE BRIGHT AND REALLY BRIGHT IDEAS

Problem: You have a collection of bright and really bright ideas as you develop a manuscript. Those ideas need only a simple explanation and not a detailed description.

How do you express those ideas, so teachers can gobble them up like dainty morsels?

Solution: Include those concepts and techniques at the end of the book and call them "Last-Minute Bright and Really Bright Ideas."

1. Flick the light off and on to get the students' attention.

2. Collect forms from students using the class list or nominal roll; this way the forms will be in alphabetical order.

3. Have the students always line up in order of their rows or their position in the classroom. This avoids butt-ins and line-up hassles.

4. When you have a popcorn day with the students, put a small hole (hole punch) in the bottom of each student's popcorn bag. This prevents the students from blowing up the bag and bursting it.

5. Start the day with ten to fifteen minutes of sharing or music.

6. When a student is in a genuine kerfuffle over one or two percent on a test—give it to her or him. Don't perspire over the diminutive entities.

7. Use a complaint box in the classroom. Situations will be expressed that would not come verbally. Often problems brought to your attention this way can be solved in a more discreet manner.

8. When a substitute is to teach your class, have the students place their names on a card that is taped to the corner of their desks.

9. Develop a borrow box for extra pencils, geometry supplies and so forth.

10. Have at least one bulletin board full of cartoons and positive one-line jokes. Students and roving Directors of Education will enjoy reading them.

11. Use sticky notes to keep track of daily circumstances. Collect these at the end of the day for your records, if you need to.

12. Read the "fact of the day" to younger students as the day finishes, so when parents ask, "What did you learn today?" they will have a fact to tell them.

13. Instead of giving someone a hand-clap applause, give a boot-stomping applause. This works especially great with band students who are holding their instruments.

14. If it is possible, bring a student's marks from the previous year to the parent-teacher conferences.

15. Write a catchy saying or joke on the board each day. Students will arrive early to read it.

16. To increase alertness, have students write their name in the air with their nose, thumb or big toe.

17. Give out "F's" for those first finished with quality work. Make ten F's worth a prize.

18. To instantly stop students from talking, tell them to quickly put their hands in the air.

© 1996 by The Center for Applied Research in Education

NOTES

NOTES

NOTES

NOTES